# GLOBALIZATION, NATIONALISM, AND IMPERIALISM

# GLOBALIZATION, NATIONALISM, AND IMPERIALISM

## A New History of Eastern Europe

*James W. Peterson and Jacek Lubecki*

Central European University Press
Budapest–Vienna–New York

©2023 James W. Peterson and Jacek Lubecki

*Published in 2023 by*
Central European University Press

Nádor utca 9, H-1051 Budapest, Hungary
Tel: +36-1-327-3138 or 327-3000
E-mail: ceupress@press.ceu.edu
Website: www.ceupress.com

All rights reserved. No part of this publication may be reproduced,
stored in a retrieval system, or transmitted,
in any form or by any means, without the permission of the Publisher.

ISBN 978-963-386-599-6 (hardback)
ISBN 978-963-386-602-3 (ebook)

**Library of Congress Cataloging-in-Publication Data**
Names: Lubecki, Jacek, author. | Peterson, James W., author.
Title: Globalization, nationalism, and imperialism : a new history
of eastern Europe / By James W. Peterson and Jacek Lubecki.
Description: Budapest, Hungary ; New York, NY : Central European
University Press, 2023. | Includes bibliographical references and index.
Identifiers: LCCN 2023016263 (print) | LCCN 2023016264 (ebook) |
ISBN 9789633865996 (hardback) | ISBN 9789633866023 (pdf)
Subjects: LCSH: Globalization--Europe, Eastern. | Nationalism--Europe, Eastern. |
Imperialism--Europe, Eastern. | Security, International--Europe, Eastern. |
Europe, Eastern--Politics and government. | BISAC: POLITICAL SCIENCE /
International Relations / General
Classification: LCC JN96.A58 L83 2023 (print) | LCC JN96.A58 (ebook) |
DDC 327.47--dc23/eng/20230421
LC record available at https://lccn.loc.gov/2023016263
LC ebook record available at https://lccn.loc.gov/2023016264

# Contents

List of Tables         *vii*

**1 Introduction**         **1**
James W. Peterson and Jacek Lubecki

*Nationalism, Imperialism, and Globalization in the Shaping of
   Eastern Europe   1*
*Background of Theories   9*

**2 Dialectics of Globalization: Empires and Nationalism**     **13**
Jacek Lubecki

*Control by Empires Prior to WW I, 1815–1914   13*
*Emergence of Nation-States after 1918   29*
*Nazi/Fascist Empire, 1930s and 1940s   43*
*Communist Empire, 1945–89   49*
*Post-communist Expressions of Nationalism
   after 1989   64*

**3 Liberalism and Anti-Liberalism**         **69**
Jacek Lubecki

*The Spread of Liberalism and Its Discontentment   69*
*Successes of Liberalism and Persistence
   of Anti-liberalism   77*
*Conclusion: Eastern Europe between Nationalism
   and Globalization   91*

**4 Ethnic Challenges from Within and Without**     **93**
James W. Peterson

*Ethnic Warfare and Conflict within the States   93*
*Migratory Pressures from the External Environment   104*
*Theoretical Conclusion   112*

**vi**      **Contents**

5   **Domestic and Global Security Challenges**      **113**
James W. Peterson

*Terrorist Threats inside the State   113*
*Russian Imperial Challenges after Crimea Takeover, 2014   122*
*Theoretical Conclusion   133*

6   **The Cloud of COVID-19 as a Global Pressure on the
Region and Its Individual States, 2020 and After**      **135**
James W. Peterson

*Key Historical Differences   135*
*Impact of COVID-19 on Democratic Ratings   136*
*Selected Case Studies of Political and Administrative Decisions
during the 2020–22 Virus   137*
*Election Outcomes during the Crisis Years   140*
*Theoretical Conclusion   142*

7   **Conclusion: Imperialism, Globalization, and Nationalism
in Eastern Europe in the Twenty-First Century**      **143**
James W. Peterson

*Imperialism   144*
*Globalization   147*
*Nationalism   149*
*Theoretical Conclusions   152*

*Bibliography*      *153*
*Index*      *160*

# List of Tables

| | | |
|---|---|---|
| 3.1 | Average economic per capita growth, 1990–98 | 71 |
| 3.2 | Relative strength of anti-liberalism in Eastern Europe, 2010–22 | 81 |
| 3.3 | Eastern European and neighboring countries on Transparency International Index, 2021 | 87 |
| 4.1 | Number of refugees admitted by states in the region of Ukraine, 2022 | 111 |
| 5.1 | East European casualties in Afghanistan | 117 |
| 5.2 | Defensive capabilities of Eastern European states, Russia, and Ukraine in 2022 | 131 |

# Chapter 1

# INTRODUCTION

*JAMES W. PETERSON AND JACEK LUBECKI*

## Nationalism, Imperialism, and Globalization in the Shaping of Eastern Europe

With the Russian invasion of Ukraine in February 2022, issues of security have once more become paramount in Eastern Europe. The Russian shadow constitutes a new form of imperial pressure on the region from the Baltic Sea in the north to the Black Sea in the south. Some observers would even compare the current Russian attitudes to those maintained in their imperial past. For example, the Association for Slavic, East European, and Eurasian Studies (ASEEES) has called for a year-long study in the "de-colonization" of the field in its *News Net* publication (May 26, 2022). There will be less attention on the Russian interpretation and more on the richness of the cultures and political systems of the East European and Eurasian peoples. In that way, the field of study will "de-center" its thrust and encourage projects that rely less on Russian influence and interpretations. East European reactions to the new Russian imperialism take nationalist forms that aim at the preservation of their own traditions and, of course, territorial space. This case study pulls together the threads of this book and is one major and current illustration of how globalism, imperialism, and nationalism have tugged at the ends and corners of Eastern Europe for decades and even centuries.

Following Hardt and Negri's turgid but seminal *Empire*, the key distinction that we make in our book is one between imperialism and "empire" of capitalist globalism and globalization (Hardt and Negri 2000). Imperialism is based on a logic of broad and expanding territorial control enforced by multinational states, which, as we conventionally understand since the Peace of Westphalia, are

# Introduction

sovereign and control their boundaries, at least potentially, against transnational flows of people, goods, and ideas. This control was not necessarily enforced by the dominant empires of the nineteenth century, which, to the contrary, allowed for relatively unimpeded transnational flows during the period that we often call "the first age of globalization."

The logic of globalism and globalization[1] is different from the logic of imperialism: the former ignores or transcends political boundaries, as it is a process of increasing transnational movement of wealth, goods, people, and ideas in pursuit of its own inner imperatives, such as accumulation of capital or ideological diffusion despite and against the logic of statist territorial control (Heilbroner 1986; Keohane and Nye 2000). In our case, the contrasting logics of imperialism and globalization were not necessarily so clear during the "long nineteenth century" but became clear when the "second generation" of empires—the fascist and communist ones—descended on Eastern and East Central Europe between 1939 and 1989.

Among these neo-empires, the brief Nazi/fascist one, with its chief enemy defined by Hitler as "Jewish internationalism,"[2] was based on explicitly and self-consciously pursued anti-globalist logic of economic autarky coupled to racism: a desire for demographic and ideological separation between "Aryans" and "non-Aryans" (Jackel 1981). The communist version of anti-globalism was based, in turn, on a paradox and contradiction whereby an essentially globalist

---

1 Globalism can be defined as either ideology or the reality of transnational integration based on inter-continental flows of wealth, ideas, goods, and people. Globalization is the process of increasing density and speed of transnational flows and, therefore, of networks of independence at transcontinental distances (Keohane and Nye 2000). The terms "globalism" and "globalization" in some contexts are interchangeable, in some not. For instance, we can imagine a form of nationalism or imperialism that accepts the existing level of transnational flows into a given territorial state, but does not want for them to expand. That nationalism would be anti-globalization, but not necessarily anti-globalist.

2 Reduction of World War II (WWII) imperialism in the region to just Nazism and communism is probably inappropriate, as it ignores Italian imperial ambition in the Balkans. The question of Hungarian revisionism and its actual success of recreating the pre-1914 imperial Hungarian Kingdom during the 1938–41 period presents a special case here, as Horthy's Hungary was not fascist, but was clearly imperial.

## Introduction

("proletarian internationalist") ideology of Marxism-Leninism was grafted onto one of the most brutally controlling and territorially bound militaristic imperial states: the Soviet Union. Just as nineteenth-century empires crumbled in 1917–18, fascist and communist imperialisms failed against forces of globalization in 1989–91, again aided by the third force in our dialectics: nationalism.

By now it should be clear to our readers that we see nationalism and globalization not necessarily as opposites, but rather as a dialectical pair that helps and abets each other, while being in seeming contradiction. If we take the conventional definition of nationalism as an ideology that a culturally defined community should pursue the ideal of a separate and sovereign nation-state, both globalism's and nationalism's enemy is territorial imperialism of multinational empires. However, within the logic of nationalism there is also a potential for anti-globalism. After all, the ideal of statist territorial control is common to both imperialism and nationalism: both seek to control transnational flows and protect the substance of either a nation or an "imperial ideal" contained within a given state border.

In our specific context and in practice, though, nationalism necessarily represents small- or medium-sized states and nations that cannot really aspire to such features of imperialism as economic autarky or grandiose notions of conquest and domination of other states or nations. Most nineteenth- and twentieth-century Eastern European nationalisms simply aspired for their respective nation-states to be created and accepted into an otherwise globalized community of liberal-democratic nations. Even today's twenty-first-century Eastern and East Central European nationalisms, such as Orbán's ideal of "illiberal democracy," are essentially "defensive" and only ambiguously opposed to globalism, but definitely opposed to the European Union (EU) perceived as a form of imperialism. In this respect, the Russian war against Ukraine can be interpreted as a bizarre and atavistic return to a logic of territorial imperialism. Alternatively, with Putin's denial that Ukrainian people exist at all we can see the war as an attempt to create Russia as something it has never been: a nation-state of Russian people, cleansed of "others," not a multinational empire.

Our ambition in this book is not to create yet another history of nationalism and of international relations of Eastern and Central Europe—there is no shortage of good books on this topic, most recently, John Connelly's *From Peoples into Nations* (2020). Instead, we intend to use a conceptually informed account to discover the patterns and logics that illuminate long-term dialectics of Eastern and East Central European history and allow us to see the current events of the region in a broader historical and conceptually informed context.

In addition to illuminating the broader dialectics of globalization, nationalism, and imperialism, our book also takes advantage of different theories that illuminate the interaction between these four forces. First, nationalism is illuminated by "legacy theory," which sees the essence of nationalism in an imagined reconstruction of the national past as a function of a nation's political aspirations. Second, "divergence and convergence theory" looks at transnational flows that bring states and nations into either an ideological and institutional convergence or divergence. Such convergence, for instance, was created by the hegemony of political and economic liberalism in Eastern Europe in the 1990s, while forces of divergence are more visible in the 2010s, with Poland and Hungary asserting their nationally distinctive and illiberal ideologies. Third, a study of domestic pressures, which when created can impact the decision-making processes within both national and imperial states, can be called the "public policy formation theory."[3] Fourth, the classical "realist theory" calls for a sharp focus on state interests as defined by the international environment and the imperatives of power and survival, but with the protection of national or imperial values and interests at its core. Realism operates in an especially acute form when new nation-states receive jarring pressures from minority ethnic groups within and from hostile states on their borders.

Chapter 2 takes a long political and historical perspective on many issues that form the essence of struggles among globalization, imperialism, and nationalism in the region. Prior to World War I

---

3 Within this broad theory, one can also incorporate various policy formation conceptualizations, such as the "systems theory" or "public management theory."

## Introduction

(WWI), the Ottoman, Russian, German, and Austro-Hungarian empires held sway over the entire region. The eruption of nationalism at the end of WWI resulted in the setting-up of nation-states that preserved their independence from larger outside forces for two full decades. However, the Nazi Empire represented an especially virulent portrayal of the logic of anti-globalist imperialism backed by horrific violence. The Soviet defeat of Nazi Germany brought about a short and ambiguous interlude after the war of restoration of democratic systems but then a harsh elimination of them with the communist take-overs soon thereafter. The failure of contradictory and paradoxical Soviet imperialism in the 1989 revolutions made clear the power of dialectics that characterized the region for at least a century.

In Chapter 3, the main features of the post-communist era emerge. On the one hand, the forces of globalization and liberalism immediately consumed many of the post-communist states, and often bore the hallmarks of western-style free markets. Leaders of the newly freed states had a tough choice to make. Should they move quickly to a free market system, with all the dislocations this entailed for groups that had become habituated to the provision of basic services, such as education and medical care, on a relatively equitable basis, although under communist controls? On the other hand, the elites might take the slow approach to the move to free market capitalism in order to preserve a modicum of economic stability for the important groups in the population. States differed in their choices, as domestic and international pressures pulled post-communist states in different directions. States such as the Czech Republic, Poland, and Estonia, which took the approach of a quick transition to capitalism, achieved notable results after a few stressful, transitional years. At the same time, militant, illiberal nationalism reared its head in many of these states as a counter-reaction to the shocks connected with the quick move to a western market approach: that was especially the situation in the less economically developed Balkans, but also in Belarus and Ukraine. In some cases, the result was the incorporation of an autocratic form of government that counteracted the essence of economic liberalism.

**6**  **Introduction**

Chapter 4 looks at both domestic ethnic struggles and outside pressures from migration, and enhances the growing understanding of national and global pressures on state leaders. The ethnic challenges have been continuous since the start of the post-communist era. At the beginning of the period, many observers expected that a lengthy period of continuous peace would replace the constant tension and struggle between West and East. Instead, the Balkan Wars erupted and required NATO air strikes to bring them to an end. Other ethnic tensions simmered within the region and occasionally came to the surface. They included the role of Russian minorities within the Baltic states, the rights of the Turkish minority in Bulgaria, and Muslim/Albania battles against Slavic majorities in Macedonia and Serbia. These challenges have a dual impact as expressions of nationalism, for they weaken the nation-state but also express nationalistic pressures from key minority groups within the countries. Migration has brought global pressures over the years. In earlier times, the exodus of Roma peoples into key Eastern European states often led to misunderstandings in the way they differed from the established populations who had lived there for centuries. The Middle East migration of the 2015–16 period led to sharply nationalistic reactions within Eastern European states, as again the newcomers were very different in background, and locals feared they may conspire with outside Muslim extremists and even terrorists. Finally, most refugees from the Russo-Ukrainian War of 2022 came west and settled in key states of the region. This was a much smoother inclusion process due to the enormous sympathy for them in spite of the pressure they then put on local economies and educational systems.

As explored in Chapter 5, security challenges were also paramount in the region, and as to be expected, they bore the traces of both national and global pressures. After the emergence of al Qaeda and ISIS, with their attacks on western countries, each state in Eastern Europe began to take precautions and erect barriers in case attacks occurred on their own soil. These protective security arrangements addressed subterranean networks that may have had linkages to suspicious individuals within their own countries. It was also necessary to keep an eye on persons who had been to

## Introduction

countries such as Syria and Iraq in order to make sure they had not established dangerous connections in those states and then returned home to link up with terrorism. It is also true that domestic protests occasionally took place against the growing authoritarianism of certain states in the area, and at times the crack-down on such protests also verged on violence. A principal global security pressure in the previous three decades had been the uncertainty about Russian intentions and plans towards the region. A full fourteen states within Eastern Europe had become NATO members in the 1999–2021 period, and this was an alliance that had been established against potential Soviet aggressiveness during the Cold War. While the Russian threat was not the predominant motivation for the countries of the region to join NATO (fear of instability and wars of Yugoslavian succession were more important), and terrorism dominated the new NATO members' concerns between 2000 and 2005, Russia started to loom large in the alliance's considerations after Putin's famous Munich speech in 2007 and the Georgian war of 2008. Russian cyberwarfare against the three Baltic states; its manipulation of its oil and natural resources at the expense of states that had become dependent on it; occasional responses to western defensive tactics through upgraded military capabilities in its exclave of Kaliningrad; and flirtation with China as a wedge against Eastern European participation in both the EU and NATO: all had kept Eastern European states and their leaders perpetually on their back heels.

However, the Russian attacks into Ukraine in 2014 and 2022 raised outside security threats from Russia to a new level. The attack on Crimea in 2014 played on domestic conflict within Ukraine between the dominant Ukrainian and minority Russian populations, but it also supported ethnic Russian military attacks within Crimea and secretly introduced military forces from Russia proper into the conflict. The West did not accept the Russian occupation and declaration of the key Black Sea territory as a Russian Republic. However, the Russian threat to Eastern Europe was doubly compounded when they attacked Ukraine from several directions in 2022. If Moscow could, without evidence, declare Ukrainian a fascist state that needed Russian control, what might happen in the Baltics, Poland, or Moldova? Thus, the vicious Russian attack and countless casualties were a powerful sign that the shadow of a potentially violent storm hovered over their lands as well and constituted a considerable global security threat.

Finally, COVID-19, the subject of Chapter 6, was an overwhelmingly powerful global factor that sharply intruded into and impinged on all the states in Eastern Europe in 2020 and after. Regimes within the nations sought to control the virus in countless ways, and the political and administrative tactics varied in their nature as well as in their impact on the citizens of the states themselves. Democracy ratings during the crisis were volatile, as they improved in some but declined in others. For instance, Estonia had enjoyed high democracy ratings for decades but experienced a decline during the COVID crisis. In contrast, Serbia's reputation during and after the Balkan Wars had sunk to dark depths but rose to a respectable level during the health crisis of the early 2020s. Many elections were held during the pandemic, and in some cases the disease had no impact on their outcomes, such as in the Czech Republic in 2021. However, in others, the administration's general handling of the crisis did impact election outcomes and that was true in Kosovo. Clearly, this case study reflects a considerable tension between forces for globalization and nationalism.

Overall, this book endeavors to make a significant contribution to the traditional duality of globalization and nationalism, and its theories and case studies sharpen our understanding of the continuing impact of this tension on both the region and individual states of Eastern Europe. There is a big difference in the interaction of those two forces between the earlier twentieth century and the earlier twenty-first century. Old empires still existed, as did forces of globalization, at the beginning of WWI, and they differed from twenty-first-century pressures such as China's vigorous export policy or the flow of refugees from the Middle East into or through Eastern Europe. Nationalism was very different as well, for the focus was on carving out new democratic states in 1918 and 1989, whereas in the twenty-first century, its dynamics included populism and authoritarianism. Subsequently, the dialectics of nationalism and globalization took seemingly different forms in the past than in the

**Introduction** 9

present. Differences and similarities of historical dialectics are precisely what our book seeks to illuminate. Just as new states emerged out of the rubble heap of WWI, so did they in the first two decades after the end of the Cold War in many parts of Eastern Europe. In addition, just as Germany's brutal expansion commenced more than two decades after the end of WWI, so did Russia's a little more than two decades after 1989.

## Background of Theories

Globalization, nationalism, and imperialism are intertwined concepts that can bear real fruit in comprehending the current political realities in Eastern Europe. All three have been dynamic forces within the region since at least 1848. Waves of globalization abetted the emergence of new states within the region, thus creating both order and disorder. Besides the conceptual frameworks illuminated in the first part of this chapter, it is important to examine in more detail theories pertinent to the phenomena of nationalism and globalization over many decades in Eastern Europe.

A number of formal theories can cast light on the multiple ways in which globalization forces threaten and sometimes overwhelm the growth and purposeful planning for nationalism as part of the foundations of a multitude of states. First, the "legacy theory" of nationalism is key to understanding modern nationalism as it emerged in opposition to empires, based on both reconstructed (and anachronistic) notions of past "national" glory and past resistance against empires. Second, "divergence and convergence theory" is crucial for understanding how interactions between forces of globalization and domestic political imperatives shape the actions of states, both in foreign and domestic political spheres. Third, "domestic policy formation" illuminates, from a comparative political perspective, how different domestic political forces form and shape state responses to crises and opportunities. Fourth, realism, and its accompanying notions, such as the balance of power, illuminate how international pressures of power and survival shape state actions.

## Legacy Theory: Memories of Past National Accomplishments and Resistance against Empires

Nationalism emerged as a strong force and an important part of the legacy of Eastern Europe in the second half of the nineteenth century. When independent states emerged there immediately after WWI, their foundation was a resultant form of "cultural nationalism" that eventually became a type of state religion and that offered a profound justification for the achievement of independence (Kovrig 1995, 14–15). During the communist period, expressions of nationalism emerged in particular in Poland, Hungary, and Czechoslovakia. Repression by Soviet and Warsaw Pact forces pushed the nationalist sympathies back into a somewhat hidden corner. As a result, they broke out with "an extreme negativism" after the winning of independence in 1989 and 1991. With the collapse of the Warsaw Treaty Organization (WTO) and the Council for Mutual Economic Assistance (CMEA), there was a sharp loss in state security, and nationalism helped to fill the void (Volgyes 1995, 2). Some described the nationalist explosions as a result of a "new tribalism" that fomented major human tragedies such as the Balkan Wars of the mid-1990s (Barany 1995, 113). Overall, it is hard to imagine a legacy that had such positive and negative implications for the region over more than a century and a half.

## Divergence and Convergence Theory

Why do some states in Eastern Europe diverge sharply from each other in political tactics while others converge in important ways? Divergence and convergence theory offers conclusions that help clarify these national differences. On the one hand, convergence theory in the 1990s offered the assumption that a new "liberal internationalist ideology" would probably replace the sharp divide between the communist and western democratic worlds that characterized much of the Cold War (Peterson and Lubecki 2019, 8). For instance, the NATO Partnership for Peace Plan and eventual offers of full alliance membership to the states of the region pulled all who joined in a common defense security direction. Similarly, the promise of EU membership offered commonality such as use of the Euro as a replacement for the national currencies, and as a result that alliance became a "whirlpool of convergence." In the defense area, many of the states took part in EUFOR ALTHEA as the primary tool for managing the latent conflict in Bosnia-Herzegovina after December 2, 2004. On the other hand, divergent patterns were also characteristic of state activities in the region. In defense policy, Polish commitments were considerably greater than those of the Czech Republic. In the early twenty-first century, ultra-nationalist forces emerged in most of the states, but only in Hungary and Poland did they actually take power (Peterson and Lubecki 2019, 152–59). Thus, this two-pronged theory can assist in predicting the basis of stability or continuing insecurity throughout the geographic area.

## *Domestic Policy Formation Theory*

Study of public policy theory can bear fruit in suggesting how pressures from within the nation can translate into actual foreign policies. In fact, the "domestic environment" has the potential to shape policies as much as the international atmosphere, so often does. Political socialization occurs in every state and helps produce very different cultures among them. Resulting cultural conflicts within a democratic state will force compromises at the political level that are often likely to impinge on security policy making. There may also exist a certain political polarization within the state that is rooted in contrasting views about the legitimacy of the leadership and the matter of trust in it. Governing structures also can impact the policy-making process, as some states are quite centralized while others have chosen federalist systems in which powers are shared at different levels (Kraft and Furlong 2013, 8–14). For example, responses to the 2020–21 COVID-19 crisis have sharply differed in the two types of states, with a corresponding effect on their relations with their geographic neighbors. In these ways, the power of nationalism is quite varied in its expressions but generally able to affect the policy-making process.

## *Realism: Protection of National Values and State Interests*

Traditionally, realist theory has possessed a sharp focus on protection of state interests defined as power. Hans Morgenthau expressed this emphasis as the only logical one after the world had weathered its enormous stresses and difficulties during the WWII period, and many other states plugged into its perspectives and implications. In fact, the flood of global pressures in the new century led to the emergence of a revised realist theory that accommodated a broader perspective. National interests and values were still vital, but there needed to be a balance between them and regional and global factors. Nations could not defend against al Qaeda and ISIS by themselves and with only a narrow preoccupation with their own vital, state interests. Work with other states became a prerequisite in order truly to enhance their own security (Peterson 2017, 31–33).

# Chapter 2

# DIALECTICS OF GLOBALIZATION: EMPIRES AND NATIONALISM

*JACEK LUBECKI*

## Control by Empires Prior to WW I, 1815–1914

The year 1815 found Eastern and East Central Europe, defined as the zone of Europe between the Russian and Germanic worlds, firmly in the grip of four great territorial empires: Habsburg, Prussian, Russian, and Ottoman. These were rooted in sixteenth–eighteenth-century territorial expansion and controlled by absolutist regimes that successfully beat back the challenge of ambiguously progressive and exploitative Napoleonic imperialism. The empires, while politically reactionary, were inevitably forced to participate in the process of global development as the price of non-progress was a military, economic, and social decline, and therefore, a defeat in the imperial power game. They also had to face up to ideological realities created by the eighteenth-century Enlightenment: liberalism and the existence and spread of modern nationalism, especially its liberal variety. The fact that Western European powers engaged in a process of overseas expansion, subjugation, and sometimes extermination of non-European peoples—colonialism——was not lost on native populations of Eastern Europe, subject to similar processes. In other words, Eastern Europe was intermeshed in globalization.

The imperative of economic development was a crucial consideration for all nineteenth-century states that hoped to survive in their realist competitive international environment, but especially for Eastern European empires, which stood on militarism, territorial expansion (chiefly Russia and Prussia), or a defense of previously acquired territories (Habsburg and the Ottoman empires). The examples of Western Europe—England, undergoing industrial development and reviving its global empire after the setback suffered with American secession; and France, which just flexed its imperial muscle in Europe using energies of social and cultural modernization—could not be ignored. When in 1854–55 France and England confronted Russia, the social and technological advancement of the former and backwardness of the latter was one of the reasons for Russia's humiliating defeat in the Crimean War, thus sparking an abolition of serfdom and a new round of Russia's modernization. When, in turn, Russia confronted the Ottomans in 1877–78, a similar dynamics operated in Russia's favor. It was becoming ever clearer that military power stood on economic power and social modernization, and power, in the modern context, could not be preserved by reactionary forms of social and economic life.

The empires, to survive, had to allow forces of globalization to penetrate them, but these forces undermined the empires, as the socioeconomic modernization sparked modern nationalism. In this respect, a similarity of Eastern European experience to Western European empires' nineteenth-century overseas colonial experience and its failure in the twentieth century becomes obvious. Ideas, institutions, and technologies coming from the Western part of the continent, which in itself was a part of a globalizing world, thus diffused into Eastern Europe. This process of convergence of Eastern European states was motivated in part by the imperial realism and in part, a result of globalization. In other words, forces of ideological and structural convergence operated in the nineteenth century just as much as they operated in 1945–89 or post-communist Eastern Europe.

Sustained economic growth is a modern phenomenon that reached Eastern Europe in the nineteenth century. According to Angus Maddison, per capita growth in the region was 0.63 percent between 1820 and 1870, doubling to 1.31 percent between 1870 and 1913 (Madison 2006, 183–188) . This happened despite (or because of) the region's exploding population, which doubled between 1820 and 1913, from. 36.5 million to 79.5 million. Meanwhile, the overall wealth of the region (adjusted to 1990 dollars) sextupled between 1820 and 1913, from $23,149 million to $121,559 million.

## Globalization: Empires and Nationalism

The most explosive growth of the economy and population in the region happened between 1870 and 1913,[1] during the so-called "second industrial revolution," driven by application of science in industry and growth in steel, electrical and chemical industrial, and transportation sectors (Maddison 2006, 180–87; Persson 2010, chapter 6). This growth was also a function of the heyday of "first globalization," as volume of merchandize exports from Eastern Europe and Russia[2] increased on average annually by 3.27 percent between 1870 and 1913, so that by 1913, merchandise exports represented 2.5 percent of the region's gross domestic product (GDP) (Maddison 2006, 127). As a result, in 1913 Eastern Europe and Russia achieved their region's historically highest proportion of the global GDP, at 13.1 percent,[3] as compared, for instance, to Western Europe's 33.5 percent for the same period (Maddison 2006).

Economic modernization is always accompanied by a social one, indicated by such phenomena as urbanization, literacy, or increasing life expectancy. This modernization occurred in Eastern Europe especially rapidly after 1870. Clearly resulting from the wholesale abolition of serfdom, which persisted in the region until the 1860s,[4] the region's social development indicators showed a significant upwards surge. For instance, on the eve of WWI literacy rates in the Austrian part of the Austro-Hungarian Empire were around 85 percent, while in the Hungarian part they were closer

---

1 Growth was even higher in the 1950-73 period, when the recovery from WWII and initial developmental energy of Marxism-Leninism resulted in very high rates of growth and modernization (Maddison 2006). By the end of this period, in 1973, the Eastern European and Russian share of global GDP was also 13.1 percent.
2 A separate figure for Eastern Europe is not available.
3 Conversely, in 1998 it was 5.3 percent (Maddison 2006, 127) behind every other region of the world except Africa, reflecting a generalized economic crisis that followed the fall of communism.
4 Serfdom/corvée was abolished in the German/Prussian territories in the late eighteenth and early nineteenth centuries, in 1848 in the Habsburg Empire, and in the 1860s in Russia. In the Ottoman Empire, abolition of serfdom varied dramatically from territory to territory; it happened as early as the mid-eighteenth century in Moldova and Wallachia, and as late as 1878 (at independence) in Bulgaria. In Bosnia, elements of serfdom persisted until 1918.

to 50 percent, thus quadrupling or tripling from around 20 percent on average in the early nineteenth century (Judson 2021; Vincent 2000, 9–10). In the meantime, the 1897 Russian census estimated the literacy rates as 33 percent for men and 14 percent for women, but in 1913 68 percent of military conscripts in Russia were reported literate. Of course, there were dramatic differences between different parts of the region: by 1900 unified Germany was reporting over 90 percent literacy rates, while in the European areas of the Ottoman Empire that became independent by the 1870s literacy rates were below 20 percent (Vincent 2000, 11). The development of the region was thus unequal; it followed a clear gradient from the north and west to the east and south, the former being richer and more developed, the latter poorer and less developed. However, progress in social and economic modernization was to be noted almost everywhere and marked a decisive convergence of the region.[5]

The connection between globalization and accompanying socioeconomic modernization and nationalism is a well-known phenomenon and its dynamics operated in a classical way in Eastern Europe. On the one hand, the region's dominant empires confronted their enemies and allies in Western Europe and therefore became aware of the benefits of cultural and political unification implied in the modern ideal of a nation-state (Greenfeld 1992). This led to imperial efforts at greater cultural unification of empires, and therefore, greater oppression and efforts at deculturation of subject, non-dominant ethnicities, and cultures. These efforts, in turn, led to a backlash by these non-dominant groups, which were also becoming more nationally self-aware as a result of socioeconomic modernization (Connelly 2020, part I). As peasants moved from their rural isolation to cities, and the spread of literacy made languages and cultures of the lower classes and non-dominant groups more important, nationalisms of subordinate groups emerged and confronted empires, which began to fray and wobble between oppression and accommodation as a response. After all, the Western European and American core of globalization was sending contradictory ideologies to the East: imperial nationalisms

---

5 Some areas, for various reasons, remained isolated from this trend: one can list Albania or the Pripyat Marshes region of the Russian empire/Belorus.

## Globalization: Empires and Nationalism

preached cultural homogenization and subjugation of minorities, anti-imperial nationalisms propagated dissolution of empires, liberalism implied universally inclusive states and rights for all, while, last but not least, colonialism and racism embraced total suppression, subjugation, and even extermination of subordinate cultures and ethnicities. Ideologies of class liberation, which sometimes saw nationalisms as "bourgeois," were added to the ideological mix and confusion by the end of the nineteenth century.

We agree with John Connelly (2020) that the recent efforts of scholarship to see all nationalisms as "constructed," contingent, and, in some sense, artificial, is misguided. Eastern European subordinate nationalisms were built on objective substrata of language, religion, and political past or "legacies"; these were not "constructed" but objective existing structures. However, how various subordinate nationalisms emerged in confrontation with dominant empires was indeed subject to historical contingencies and human agency, so therefore "constructed" of sorts from these objectively existing frameworks. The changing nature of empires, the varying forces of socioeconomic modernization, and the nature of nationalisms themselves—often predicated on the political past of the respective nations—created a variety of objective circumstances and possibilities of responses, and therefore varying forms of nationalisms in the region in question.[6] A conceptually informed account of their emergence emphasizing broader patterns and contemporary relevance of the 1815–1914 period is therefore necessary.

Following our legacy theory framework, and standard histories of nationalism such as Greenfeld's (1992) and Connelly's (2020), we see institutional and political past as primary determinants of types of nationalisms that emerged in nineteenth-century Eastern Europe. One primary distinction, stripped of its initial Hegelian/

---

6 Anthony Giddens's structuration theory is the best explanation of the phenomenon in action; according to him, no social action is possible without preexisting social structures that constrain actors, but agency is possible as structures can be modified, which, in turn, constrain and empower a new set of actors (Giddens 1984). This idea is similar to the well-known notion of path-dependency.

racist connotation,[7] is between the ideal types of "historic" and "non-historic" forms of nationalism that should be re-conceptualized as "aristocratic" and "plebeian." As conceived by Hegel (and Engels afterward), "historic" nations were ones with recent traditions of statehood, and featuring, therefore, their own aristocracies, upper classes, and forms of high cultural and autonomous political life. According to Engels, Polish, Hungarian, and German nationalisms fitted that type. "Non-historic" nations were ones that lost independent statehood a long time ago, and therefore were embodied in mostly lower social strata who spoke native languages and embodied plebeian cultures. Czechs, Slovaks, Belorussians, Ukrainians, Baltic nations, Transylvania Romanians, Serbs, Bulgarians, and Macedonians would certainly fit that type. Ambiguous cases involved Croats and Romanians of Moldova and Wallachia, who were always given some form of autonomy within, respectively, the Hungarian Kingdom (a part of the Habsburg Empire since 1526) and the Ottoman Empire. Even more ambiguous in this respect were Bosnians—Islamized Slavs of the Ottoman province of Bosnia—who enjoyed a privileged status within the empire with which they identified, and Albanians, divided into an Ottomanized ruling elite and peasant masses hardly touched by modernity.

The fundamental difference between historic and non-historic types of nationalism lies not in the former's supposedly "progressive" and the latter's "reactionary" nature, as imputed by Engels in his 1848–49 writings, but in the fact that historic nationalities had to contend with extreme class and status divisions within their own nationality, and with legacies of their own recent imperialism. The Polish gentry, which until 1795 enjoyed its own state and which had dominated Polish-, Ukrainian-, and Belarusian-speaking peasant-serf masses, quickly realized that countering the occupying empires of Russia, Prussia, and Austria involved the challenge of convincing the Slavic peasants that a restoration of the Polish statehood was in their own interest. The challenge of Polish nationalism thus

---

7 For Engels, writing in the context of the 1848 revolution, "historic" nations were "revolutionary" bearers of progress whose nationalism should be supported by progressive forces, while "non-historic" people embodied backwardness and reaction, and should be suppressed. See Rosdolsky (1987).

## Globalization: Empires and Nationalism

involved bridging a class and cultural divide within the emerging modern Polish nation in the context of foreign occupation. This was hard, as the imperial elites were more than happy to appeal to Polish-speaking peasant masses against their Polish masters. In a classic case of such dynamics, a Polish gentry-led national uprising against Austrian rule in 1846 was defeated and its participants massacred by Polish-speaking peasants instigated by Austrian bureaucracy, thus making a mockery of modern Polish nationalism. Indeed, as late as in the 1920s and 1930s, in the context of a revived Polish national state, Polish peasants' conviction that the state is an alien force aimed at peasant repression and even a restoration of serfdom persisted. This resentment was doubled for Orthodox or Greek Catholic Belarusians and Ukrainians living in 1918–39 Poland, for whom the Polish state represented both national and class oppression. Only the end of WWII, when Poland lost territories inhabited by non-Polish minorities, marked the end of Polish imperial nationalism.

Similarly to the Polish case, Hungarian gentry and aristocracy embodied the autonomous tradition of the Hungarian Kingdom and maintained their political and cultural autonomy for centuries even though their own sovereign state disappeared after 1526. While resentful of the Habsburg domination and its Germanic nature, the Hungarian aristocracy also lorded over Magyar-speaking lower classes, and, more importantly, non-Magyars, mostly Slavic or Romanian peasants in the territories of the historical Hungarian Kingdom.[8] This meant that when in 1848–49 the Hungarian elite struck for independence under banners of democracy and liberalism, the Hungarian rural lower classes were less than enthusiastic for the cause of a Hungarian nation-state. Even more importantly, the non-Magyars were hostile to Hungarian nationalism and supportive of imperial Habsburg restoration. The resulting mutual massacres and ethnic cleansing campaigns that occurred in the course of the Hungarian lost war of independence were premonitions of similar events of WWI and WWII and were among the first examples of a genocidal potential of modern nationalisms. The

---

8 The one exception was Croatia, where Catholic Croats preserved some traditions of local autonomy and an indigenous elite.

**20**      **Globalization: Empires and Nationalism**

Hungarian war of independence exemplified the entire 1848–49 unsuccessful "spring of nations" when burgeoning nationalisms of Eastern Europe first proved to be incompatible with democratic liberalism, and forces of imperial reaction won.

While Polish nationalism evolved after 1846, and, by and large, successfully incorporated Polish-speaking Catholic popular masses into its realm, resulting in the creation of a modern Polish-dominated nation-state in 1918, Hungarian nationalism underwent a different transformation. By a twist of historical irony, after a dramatic defeat in the war against Prussia in 1866, the Austrian Empire turned to the Hungarian elite to rescue the failing state. This was accomplished by offering a form of limited national sovereignty to the Hungarian Kingdom within a framework of a confederate "Dual Monarchy." As a result the Hungarian part of the Dual Monarchy became the largest and most powerful, be it semi-sovereign, modern Hungarian state that existed between 1868 and 1918. By the late nineteenth century, animated by a sense of Hungarian nationalism, the Hungarian state elite launched policies of magyarization, an attempt to make all people of the country Magyar in culture and political consciousness. The aristocratic, elite-dominated, and semi-authoritarian nature of Hungarian state and society continued, which meant that nationalism was accompanied by persistent glaring class and status inequalities within the Magyar nation, and an imperial oppression of non-Magyars. When the Hungarian Kingdom was defeated in WWI, it experienced a social revolution and was stripped down to its bare Hungarian ethnic core in the Trianon Peace Treaty of 1920. Still, stark class inequalities continued in 1920–41 Hungary. This social reality was coupled to Hungarian revisionism: a blistering resentment and desire for revenge against all neighboring countries and signatories to the Treaty of Trianon: Czechoslovakia, Yugoslavia, Romania, France, and England. Hungary thus sought a restoration of its empire in alliance with Nazi Germany during WWII and was defeated as an Axis power and restored to 1920 boundaries[9] in the Paris Peace Treaty of 1947.

However, it was nationalisms of non-historic nations that numerically dominated nineteenth-century Eastern Europe. For

---

9 Minus Trans-Carpathia, annexed by Stalin to the Soviet Union.

## Globalization: Empires and Nationalism

these nations, class divisions did not exist in the sense that the nation was lower class: predominantly peasants, urban working and middle classes, and some intelligentsia, such as lower clergy. The elites were non-national: Islamized Slavs or Greek officials in the Ottoman Empire; Germanic upper classes and bureaucrats in Habsburg Bohemia; Hungarian lords and bureaucrats in Slovakia and Transylvania; Russians and Baltic Germans in Estonia and Latvia; Russian bureaucrats and Polish landowners in Lithuania; Austrian bureaucrats and Polish landowners in Austrian Galicia; and Russians and Polish landowners in Ukraine and Belarus. For these plebeian nations, the work of nationalism was, in a sense, simpler than in historic nations, since no major class divides had to be bridged; the hated "masters" were all national aliens. This work could also be infinitely more difficult: in the absence of resources provided by strong native middle classes, intelligentsia, and aristocracy, the labor of teaching and spreading national languages, cultures, and identities could be hard. In some cases, the work was almost too difficult: Belarus nationalism continued to be weak throughout the twentieth and twenty-first centuries regardless of national statehood since 1991, while the Rusyn (or Carpatho-Rusyn) nationalism is still a cultural rather than a political phenomenon.

Various circumstances favored the emergence of weaker or stronger forms of "non-historic" nationalisms. In the Czech lands, economic prosperity, which has blessed this fertile and industrious territory since the seventeenth century, translated into an economic boom by the early nineteenth century, which largely continued until 1914. This brought about a rural-urban migration and therefore Czech-speaking majorities into cities, where they met with a burgeoning Czech language and culture revival movement, which from the late eighteenth century preached a superiority of Czech language, culture, and history over the interloping, alien, and oppressive German-speaking upper classes. Led by luminaries such as František Palacký (the author of the most famous history of historical independent Bohemia), František Rigier (the leader of the early Czech national movement), and eventually, Tomáš Garrigue Masaryk (the leader of the "Young Czech" national movement, considered the "Father" of independent Czechoslovakia in 1918), the Czech national movement grew by leaps and bounds, striving for autonomy within the framework of the Habsburg/Austro-Hungarian Empire until 1914, and, increasingly, for independence during WWI. The fact that Czech speakers were the majority within the boundaries of the old Bohemian Kingdom and that the Austrian state became progressively liberalized in the course of the nineteenth century meant that the logic of democratic liberalism favored the Czech national cause, and it could be pursued peacefully. This was helped by an essentially plebeian, bourgeois nature of Czech nationalism, which, in the absence of stark class divisions within the nation, favored liberal democratic politics. A combined result of Czech plebeian nationalism and the economic prosperity of Bohemia and Moravia was the emergence of interwar Czechoslovakia as the most stable, liberal-democratic, and prosperous state of interwar Eastern Europe. Significantly, after the totalitarian interlude, the Czech positive trajectory largely reemerged after 1989 and continued after the split with Slovakia in 1992.

The Slovak national movement was similar to the Czech one by being plebeian: the masters of Slovak peasants had been Hungarian aristocrats since the Middle Ages. Like the Czechs, the Slovaks had their national revival movement in the nineteenth century, led by cultural and political luminaries such as Ján Kollár, Ľudovít Štúr, and Pavel Šafárik. However, unlike the Czechs, Slovaks remained mostly poor, Catholic, conservative, and oppressed peasants in a fairly underdeveloped Hungarian section of Austria-Hungary, where they faced an authoritarian regime bent on suppression of Slovak national identity. Liberal and democratic tradition was thus weakly developed in Slovakia: the economic basis for liberalism was lacking, while an alliance with Czech nationalism against imperial, Austro-Hungarian domination ignored essential differences between Czechs and Slovaks. When the common state of Czechs and Slovaks emerged in 1918, no amount of mutual good will could paper over the fact that the more-educated and prosperous Czechs patronized the poorer and less-developed Slovaks. Thus, Czechoslovakia dissolved first in 1938 and then in 1992. Importantly, post-WWII Slovakia, unlike Czechia, maintained its former imperial minority: while Germans were ethnically cleansed from Czechia in 1945, Hungarians remained in Slovakia, and, since 1992, they could be an object of nationalistic agitation, which did a lot to bolster the nationalist populist regime of Vladimír Mečiar. Clearly, a plebeian nationalism was no guarantee of the development of liberal democracy; when coupled to relative poverty and the presence of national "enemies," it could lead to the reverse.

Like the Czechs, Serbs lost their native aristocracy as a result of Ottoman conquest in the late Middle Ages, and were a plebeian peasant nation similar to the Slovaks. However, the tradition of statehood and of armed struggle for independence was preserved through the Orthodox Church and popular oral epics regardless of centuries of national suppression. This created a militarized and insurgent type of nationalism, which struck out for a sovereign statehood as one of the first nationalisms in Eastern Europe. The 1804–17 revolt of Serbian peasants against Ottoman rule, after a savage back-and-forth struggle, led to a Serbian de facto independent state that was formally recognized as an autonomous entity in 1830, while still subject to a formal Ottoman sovereignty, only abolished in 1878. A princely (eventually, royal) court centered on the native Obrenoviĉ dynasty took over the rule of the state, and Serbian middle classes and a military-bureaucratic elite emerged in the midst of an essentially egalitarian peasant nation with no serfdom or glaring class differences. However, given that a Serbian-speaking Orthodox population remained outside the boundaries of the state—in Ottoman-controlled Bosnia and Kosovo, Austrian Krajina, and Vojvodina, which was a part of the Hungarian Kingdom—irredentism became the chief preoccupation of Serbian nationalism, which was increasingly allied to Russia and aimed against Austria-Hungary. With the Austro-Hungarian annexation of Bosnia in 1878, Serbian nationalism was propelled to a clash with Austro-Hungarian imperialism, which eventually led to WWI. With militaristic nationalism being the nation's chief preoccupation, democratic and liberal development of Serbia was stunted—regardless of their egalitarian social structure, Serbs were more interested in the armed struggle for unity than in economic prosperity or liberal political development. This logic favored an emergence of a militarized bureaucratic elite and authoritarian politics.

Croats were western geographical neighbors of Serbs, albeit across the Habsburg-Ottoman boundaries. The fact that Croats and Serbs essentially spoke the same language (albeit written in different alphabets: Latin for the Croats and Cyrillic for the Serbs) even though the former were Catholic and the latter Orthodox was not lost on early luminaries of modern Croat nationalism. The movement, known as the Illyrian revival, found its chief luminary in Ljudevit Gaj and was in full flourish by the middle of the nineteenth century, celebrating Croat language and culture in opposition to magyarization and successfully asserting Croat national autonomy, which was never fully suppressed in the Hungarian Kingdom. By the middle of the nineteenth century, on the Serbian side, the potential unity of Serbs and Croats was asserted by the likes of Vuk Stefanović Karadžić, and the idea of Yugoslavia, a unified state of "Southern Slavs" (Yugoslavs) that, besides Serbs and Croats, would also include Slovenians and Macedonians, was born. In 1918, as a result of historical contingencies and the fall of the Austro-Hungarian Empire, the Yugoslavian Kingdom was indeed born, but inevitably dominated by Serbs who, by then, had a hundred-year-old tradition of fully independent modern statehood, unlike all other constituent nations, which had none. More importantly, Croats enjoyed some autonomy as part of Austria-Hungary, as a mostly peasant nation lacked glaring class divisions and developed a relatively liberal and democratic political culture, which clashed with Serbian centralism and authoritarianism. Just like in the case of Czechoslovakia, the cross-national alliance of Serbs and Croats was not to last.

In Europe, besides the Serbs, the Ottoman Empire controlled other Slavic proto-nations: Bosnians (Islamized Slavs), Croats in Herzegovina (Catholic Slavs), and Serbs (Orthodox Slavs) in Bosnia and Herzegovina, Orthodox Slavs in Macedonia, as well as non-Slavic Albanians, and, in the Eastern Balkans, Romanians and Bulgarians. Of these, Bulgarians and Macedonians were ethnically related and plebeian peasant nations just like Serbs, but they had to wait much longer than Serbs for national independence. For Bulgarians, after a period of national cultural revival in the nineteenth century, and unsuccessful rebellions against the Ottoman Empire, a de facto independence came as a result of the Russian-Ottoman war of

## Globalization: Empires and Nationalism

1878–79. The war was a part of a broader breakdown and shrinkage of Ottoman power in Europe, which also resulted in concession of full sovereignty to Serbia and Montenegro,[10] occupation of Bosnia by Austria-Hungary, and the emergence of independent Romania. The initial settlement of the war in the Treaty of San Stefano created a huge Bulgaria stretching from the Black Sea almost to the Adriatic (to the borders of Albania) and included Macedonia. However, other European great powers intervened in the name of balance of power, fearing a weakening of the Ottoman Empire and growth of Russian power. As a result of their intervention and the resulting 1878 Congress and Treaty of Berlin, the Ottomans kept formal control over Albania and Macedonia, while Austria-Hungary gained control over Bosnia and Sanjak of Novi Bazar (still nominally under Ottoman sovereignty). While Russian ambitions and power were tempered, in retrospect, the treaty was a failure: war, not peace, followed.

The 1878 Treaty of Berlin can be seen as the beginning of the end of the empires in Eastern Europe, with the process ending 50 years later in 1918–20 with the defeat of Russia, Germany, and Austria-Hungary and the resulting Versailles Peace Treaty of 1919. The Treaty of Berlin also set a precedent for Versailles, in a sense that great powers (in Berlin, there were six of them: Russia, Great Britain, France, Austria-Hungary, Italy, and Germany) settled boundaries and attempted to manage national conflicts in Eastern Europe on what appeared to be a compromise basis: a framework not that dissimilar to what the West/North Atlantic Treaty Organization (NATO) has tried to do in the former Yugoslavia since the 1990s. Even domestic political, humanitarian, and cultural sensibilities accompanying the treaty were similar to what we saw at the end of the twentieth century: Western public opinion was horrified by mass killing, atrocities, and ethnic cleansing

---

10 Montenegro was, for all intents and purposes, a part of Serbia, but with a tradition of independent statehood, which, due to unique geographical conditions, survived the Ottoman conquest of the region. The political distinction between Serbia and Montenegro was sufficient for Montenegrins to create their own distinct sense of nationalism and reassert it through secession from Serbia in 2006.

that accompanied the 1877–79 conflict, and great powers tried to establish early forms of "human rights protection regimes" and political settlements conducive to peace. The Versailles 1919 Peace Treaty was animated by similar sensibilities, and even post-WWII imperial settlements (embodied in decisions of Yalta, Potsdam, and the Paris Peace Treaty of 1947) can be seen as nominal attempts at similar solutions. We can see all these attempts as failures, or all as a part of a long-term process leading to peace and development.

The sovereign or semi-sovereign states that resulted from the Berlin Treaty were certainly subject to Western pressures, often backed up by internal sensibilities to establish copy-cat "Western" conservative liberal states, with constitutional monarchies and elected parliaments. As a result of this forced convergence different forms of oligarchy emerged, varying in their degrees of corruption and restrictions on democracy depending on domestic political order. Romania was a particularly negative example of this trend. Similar to Poland and Hungary, and unlike Bulgaria or Serbia in social structure, Romania emerged into independence (de facto in 1860s, de jure in 1878) with a native upper class of boyars (nobility) who kept a large portion of the land and oppressed the poor and disempowered Romanian peasant. Regardless of genuine land reforms conducted by the first leader of the country, Prince Alexander Cuza, Romania remained a land of poor peasants and a narrow and corrupt elite, which divided into "conservative" and "liberal" camps under the façade of constitutional liberal monarchy (under a Germanic prince) that offered no genuine developmental energy, or social justice for the poor. Instead, like in Hungary, negative nationalisms aimed at combating the neighboring nations: Hungary (which occupied ethnically Romanian Transylvania), Russia (which occupied Bessarabia), and Bulgaria (which occupied Dobruja) became the glue of the regime. Additionally, hatred of Jews who migrated into newly independent Romania from the Russian and Austro-Hungarian empires became an especially poisonous substitute for egalitarian politics in Romania. If one could blame "Jewish bankers" for Romanian poverty and underdevelopment, then combating the Jewish influence in Romania passed for

# Globalization: Empires and Nationalism

attempts to reform the country and to alleviate the fate of the poor majority.

Bulgaria, being a plebeian nation of egalitarian peasants, did not have Romania's social-structural disabilities, but adapted a similar political structure, with an imported Germanic monarch (from a Saxon-Coburg dynasty), the court, and a military-political clique around the monarch. Here, like in Romania and Serbia, unfinished combat with the neighbors to unify all Bulgarians into one state created negative irredentist nationalism as the dominant preoccupation. Within two decades of independence Bulgaria was embroiled in a victorious but politically inconclusive war against Serbia (1886). Then, in 1912, Bulgaria joined a League of Serbia, Montenegro, and Greece in a joint war against the Ottoman Empire, which was stripped of its last remnants of European possessions except for a tiny sliver of Thrace next to Istanbul. The war enlarged all of the participants of the anti-Ottoman League and created independent Albania, but Bulgaria was unhappy with the division of the spoils and attacked Greece and Serbia in 1913, launching a war that eventually brought Romania and the Ottoman Empire into the anti-Bulgarian coalition. Defeated, Bulgaria emerged stripped of some territories, resentful, and revisionist against its neighbors. As a result, Bulgaria entered WWI on the side of the Central Powers in 1915 and was defeated again in 1918.

On the eve of WWI the following picture of Eastern Europe can be broadly drawn: in Russia, non-Russian nationalities were all repressed, and, with the exception of Polish nationalism, all had a plebeian nature. In the Austro-Hungarian monarchy, Hungarian nationalism oppressed the non-dominant nationalities, while in the Austrian part of the empire freedom of cultural development was assured to all, but demands for political autonomy of nations continued to intensify. In Polish parts of Prussia (a part of the German Reich) the Polish minority was oppressed. However, nothing equaled the intensity and violent nature of newly emerged irredentist Balkan nation-states, whose co-national brothers and sisters still lived in the empires—such was the situation of Serbia vis-à-vis Serbs in Austria-Hungary (in Bosnia, Vojvodina, and Krajina) and Romania with regard to their ethnic brothers in Transylvania

(Hungary) and Bessarabia (Russia), as well as the Bulgarian situation with regard to Serbian-controlled Macedonia (Bulgarians considered Macedonians to be Bulgarian) and Thrace, where Bulgarians were ruled by Greece.

The collapse of the Ottoman Empire in Europe was accompanied by the emergence of militantly nationalist states, warfare, mass killing, and ethnic cleansing. Emergent nation-states fought over boundaries and identities, and militaristic forms of nationalism were hardly conducive to economic or democratic political development. European great power efforts to impose a regime of conservative liberalism and border compromises in the Balkans were futile, especially since the great powers themselves fished in the dirty waters of nationalisms looking for strategic advantage against each other. A global war developed from the Balkan cauldron.

Conceptually, we can see how forces derived from economic, social, and cultural globalization inevitably led to the rise of nationalisms of subordinate groups in the midst of Eastern European empires—the process was essentially similar to dynamics that accompanied the twentieth-century breakup of Western European overseas colonialism. However, it is also to be noted that there was no one-to-one correlation between socioeconomic modernity and the rise of successful nationalisms. To the contrary, first independent nation-states in Eastern Europe emerged in the areas that were in many ways the least modernized: first Serbia, then the rest of the Ottoman Empire. The crucial variable here was not socioeconomic modernity, but the weakness of the relatively unmodernized empire itself—to paraphrase Lenin, the successful national revolutions struck the "weakest link" of the imperial chain first. The relative strength of nationalisms was thus clearly not a simple function of socioeconomic modernity: in Serbia, oral traditions and religion provided a cultural glue that solidified an otherwise weakly modernized peasant nation. Nations that emerged in conditions of relative prosperity and modernity, like the Czechs, were strong but, prior to 1914, sought not independence but autonomy and empowerment within the existing imperial framework of Austria-Hungary. Even the fairly militant and strong Polish nationalism could not imagine itself able to defeat German and Russian empires, so mostly sought autonomy or empowerment in the context of alliance with the Austro-Hungarian Empire against Russia, or with Russia against Germany.[11]

The emerging post-imperial reality in the Balkans was typical of any post-colonial situation. It featured relatively weak states, ruled by militarized elites interested less in economic or democratic political development, and more in boundaries, national expansion, or authoritarian or semi-authoritarian internal power games. These states were also manipulated, controlled, and corrupted by external forces of European great powers as a function of their own imperial interests. Thus, while globalization sparked nationalism in Eastern Europe, imperialism and nationalisms were in their typical dialectical relationship with globalization: forces of territorial control simultaneously allowed for, but also impeded forces of de-territorialized flows of money, ideas, and goods. This logic continued in post-WWI reality.

## Emergence of Nation-States after 1918

The Central Powers won WWI in Eastern Europe before being defeated in the West, so the picture of what Austria-Hungary, Germany, the Ottoman Empire, and Bulgaria wanted in the region is clear. Besides annexation of territory, the victorious powers wanted to create puppet states: these were to be tied with Germany and Austria-Hungary into a customs union and subjugated by strings of military and political treaties. These dependent states included some form of autonomy for Baltic nations, a small Polish state in the territory previously occupied by Russia, a large Ukraine (which included some territories of today's Belarus), and, further East, a Tatar state in the Crimea and semi-independent Cossack republics in the Don area. Defeated Romania was to be left sovereign and actually gifted ex-Russian Bessarabia, but lost a part of Dobruja

---

11 Germans/Prussians were consistently and brutally too oppressive of Poles for any significant "pro-German" faction of Polish nationalism to emerge. When Germany tried to use Polish nationalism against Russia during the 1915–18 occupation of the Russian part of the Polish territories, the German efforts failed as the past oppression could not be undone.

to Bulgaria. Hungary was to be enlarged by parts of Romania and wanted to annex Bosnia, Dalmatia, and parts of Serbia. Germany was to be the imperial center of the whole "Mittleuropa" project, which also included a German annexation of parts of Belgium and France. As a result Germany was to become a new imperial center of a unified continental European economic bloc, able to compete economically and politically with the British Empire and the United States.

This imperial project failed, but was an important premonition of Hitler's vision, which was much more genocidal and brutal in Poland, Ukraine, and Russia: instead of Polish, Ukrainian, or Tatar puppet states, it envisioned extermination or enslavement of the entire peoples and German ("Aryan") settlement in thus "emptied" areas. However, in the Balkans Hitler's empire relied on allied countries, and in this respect more closely followed the earlier imperial model. Moreover, Hitler's goal was strategically the same as the German one at the end of WWI—a creation of European economic entity able to globally compete with the Anglo-Saxon powers. Defeat and destruction of interwar order in Eastern Europe had to happen before Hitler fully tried his hand, and Hitler's failure led to the establishment of Soviet hegemony in the region.

In Eastern Europe, WWI led to the destruction of the German, Russian, and Austro-Hungarian empires. While the Ottoman Empire also disintegrated as a result of the war, this was of no consequence for Eastern Europe, as the Ottomans were largely gone from Europe by 1913. The defeat of Bulgaria meant that it had to retreat to its 1913 borders—it lost its "third Balkan war." The impact of 1918 on Hungary was devastating—it was stripped to its bare ethnic core losing half of its territories, not only those inhabited by minorities but also inhabited by Hungarians. This long-term impact of WWI on Hungarians continues to this day. Austria was stripped to its ethnic core and forbidden to be unified with Germany. The whole settlement was established and policed by Western Powers, especially France and England, in alliance with newly created Eastern European states and against the defeated states.

On the other hand, several new sovereign states emerged: Poland, Yugoslavia, Latvia, Lithuania, Estonia, and Czechoslovakia. While

## Globalization: Empires and Nationalism

these states represented the fulfillment of nationalist aspirations of some nations—Poles in Poland, Czechs in Czechoslovakia, and Serbs in Yugoslavia—it did not satisfy other nations. Slovaks, Slovenians, Ukrainians, Belarusians, Croats, Macedonians, Rusyns, Bosnians, and others emerged without their own states, even though their status improved in most cases and some were given the status of nominally co-equal titular nations (Slovaks in Czechoslovakia, Croats in Yugoslavia). As many historians of the region (recently, John Connelly, and Joseph Rothschild in his classic 1974 work) rightly noticed, these new states were, in a sense, mini-empires (Rothschild 1974). Especially Poland, Czechoslovakia, and Yugoslavia were multinational states with substantial non-dominant minorities, many of whom felt deprived of their national aspirations. This alone created conditions not conducive to the flourishing of democratic liberalism in the region. Additionally, within and around the region there were revisionist states bent on destruction of post-WWI boundaries and order: the Soviet Union, with its militant ideology and imperial vision, and Germany, which vacillated between acceptance of the liberal status quo and radical revisionism until 1933, Hungary, and Bulgaria.

The West, through the Versailles Peace Treaty 1919 settlement and a series of follow-up treaties and institutions, supported an order based on economic and political liberalism in the region. By the early 1930s liberalism crumbled across the region and the world. Liberal democracies failed in every country of Eastern Europe except Czechoslovakia, while the liberal economic order largely disintegrated across the world. The failure of liberalism, however, as the newest historical works of Adam Tooze and Zara Steiner make clear, was not predetermined, but a result of particular decisions and contingencies (Steiner 2007; Tooze 2014). Indeed, a fair reading of the region's interwar history shows that the failure of liberalism was chiefly the function of the West's own disintegration and collapse in the Great Depression, as well as revisionist powers' quest for new empires in Eastern Europe. Liberal order in Eastern Europe was chiefly killed from without, not within. Indeed, as I will show, many domestic political forces in the region supported a liberal and democratic order despite, not because of,

## Globalization: Empires and Nationalism

the region's difficult objective circumstances, which will be covered first.

The war was far more devastating in Eastern Europe than in Western Europe. As the front rolled back and forth in Polish, Serbian, Bulgarian, and Romanian territories, the total war stamped a zone of desolation across large swathes of the region. Additionally, a ruthless economic exploitation of Eastern Europe by warring powers and a deliberate destruction of property and infrastructure by retreating Russia added to the material destruction. In Serbia, Austro-Hungarian practices bordered on genocide, but a willful brutality of all sides in the Balkans was stunning. Additionally, the Great War was followed by several smaller armed conflicts that affected the region after 1918 and at least until 1923. As Russia experienced a liberal democratic revolution in February 1917 and a Bolshevik one in October 1917, Russian territories fell to revolutionary violence and civil wars. Hungary succumbed to a similar revolution in 1919, which resulted in a Hungarian Bolshevik-style regime battling Czechs, Slovaks, Romanians, Serbs, and the French, as well as the domestic forces of counter-revolution. Poles, Finns, Estonians, Latvians, and Lithuanians won independence in the course of multi-sided warfare. In the Balkans, the end of the war was accompanied by massacres, ethnic cleansing, and warfare too, which meant that the region was almost constantly at war between 1911 and 1923. The destruction and brutality of post-WWI conflicts added to the one created by the Great War. As a result, the region emerged economically devastated and suffered a developmental setback. Figures provided by the Maddison Project make it clear that the average per capita GDP of the region shrunk almost by half, from $2,283 in 1910 to $1,343 in 1920 (Maddison Project 2020).[12] That was a far greater proportional economic setback than the one that resulted from WWII and might well be the worst such episode suffered by any region of the world in modern history.[13]

12 This figure includes Eastern Europe and Russia, as no separate statistics for Eastern Europe are given.
13 The population losses from WWII were far greater, though, which partially explains why the per capita GDP was less affected by the second war. Indeed, between 1910 and 1920 the population of the region grew by 34 million,

## Globalization: Empires and Nationalism

WWI made it clear that the order of globalization depended on political and economic institutions sustained by early forms of global cooperation: the Gold Standard, centered on British banking, and the global regime of conservative liberalism, which included creation of parliamentary regimes that honored international debts, issued and honored governmental bonds, and maintained stable currencies. All pre-WWI empires and newly emerging Balkan states fitted into this international system, even though it was only weakly institutionalized. WWI suspended this international economic system, while the war's outcomes created dramatic economic imbalances that eventually killed economic globalization. Most importantly, France and Great Britain emerged with a massive external debt to the United States, and large monetary overhangs as the countries printed money to pay for the war, with the Gold Standard being suspended. Additionally, the Russian economy collapsed and then left the global capitalist system under the Bolshevik regime, fully reneging on its international economic obligation, mostly to France. The victors of the war, in retrospect, chose the worst possible course of dealing with the post-war crisis: the United States demanded the full repayment of French and British war debt, while the French and the British put the onus on sustaining the system on German war reparations.

The 1920s economic and international diplomacy between great powers was all focused on dramatic efforts to restore both the Gold Standard and liberal order, while maintaining the debt *cum* war reparations scheme. By 1929 the onset of the Great Depression made the efforts doubly complicated. At that point the most far-sighted actors in the game, such as the French Foreign Minister Aristide Briand, could see that only a concerted system of international cooperation involving a voluntary debt cancelation by the United States, and a full rehabilitation and integration of Germany into a unified European economy could save the liberal order (Tooze 2014, 517). However, the US Congress insisted on sanctity of the debt, and the entire system crumbled (Tooze 2014, 493–98). By 1934 Germany was under Hitler and

---

while between 1940 and 1950, it shrunk by 23 million. Again, the figures include both Eastern Europe and Russia/the Soviet Union.

unilaterally refused to pay reparations, while France and England refused to pay the debt to the United States (Tooze 2014, 502–7). The Gold Standard disintegrated, currencies freely floated against each other, and, as countries pursued mercantilist economic policies, global trade shrunk. The first age of globalization was over, and worse was to come.

The pre-1914 imperial order in Eastern Europe was economically relatively open to transnational flows, which explains the fast economic progress made by the region. The new postwar political boundaries forced dramatic readjustments to national economies of the countries, and created new obstacles to trade, often reinforced by multiple conflicts between newly emerging countries. Significantly, Eastern Europeans largely failed to establish a region-wide system of economic and political cooperation, while the West, unable to manage its own inner economic relationships, was largely helpless in inducing such cooperation in the periphery. As a result, growth in the international trade of Eastern Europe and the Soviet Union was cut by half in the 1913–50 period as compared to 1870–1913, shrinking from 3.37 percent average annual growth to 1.43 percent. For the entire world, the growth for the same periods shrunk from 3.4 percent to 0.9. This was the age of de-globalization.

If the interwar period was economically so dismal, one can indeed wonder why in 1989 Eastern Europeans, newly liberated from the imperial yoke of the Soviet rule, celebrated the 1920s and 1930s as their lost "golden age" of freedom. A more sober assessment should have been, indeed, that trouble was coming in 1989, and, in many ways the 1990s were a dialectical repetition of the 1920s in the brutality of economic adjustment and wars that followed the crumbling of the imperial order. However, the picture is far more complicated, and there were reasons to celebrate the liberation in both the post-1918 and post-1989 periods. One reason has already been stated: the crumbling of the imperial order in both periods marked the national liberation for many nations, which in the logic of nationalism is the supreme value, worth its economic price and even price in lives. Second, in both cases the revolutions were not just national but also internal political ones; as a result of WWI the new national

# Globalization: Empires and Nationalism

states emerged as full-blown liberal democracies,[14] featuring largely unfettered free elections based on universal suffrage and therefore empowerment of the lower classes, which challenged the region's conservative and oppressive social hierarchies. The image of the 1920s as an age of freedom was therefore not a myth. Then, when liberal democracies crumbled in the region in the 1930s they were nowhere replaced by totalitarian or fascist regimes, but rather by semi-authoritarian regimes that paid at least some respect to liberal norms. Compared to the genocidal and totalitarian nightmares of Nazi fascism and Soviet communism, the 1920s and even 1930s were indeed an age of freedom.

To remind the reader: not one of the pre-1914 empires was a liberal democracy, even though all of them, including Russia after 1904 and the Ottoman Empire since 1876, paid some respects to liberal principles, featured elections, and civil societies, and can therefore fairly be characterized as semi-authoritarian regimes. Likewise, the newly emerging nation-states in the Balkans were not liberal democracies—regardless of their otherwise egalitarian social structures they were de facto ruled by narrow military-bureaucratic elites centered on their respective monarchs and their courts. Elections existed in all these countries, but did not truly determine who was in possession of executive power. Even universal manhood suffrage was a relatively recent rarity in the region, with the exception of Germany when it was introduced in 1871. Universal secret male suffrage was introduced in the Austrian part of the Austro-Hungarian Empire in 1907, but this was not extended to the Hungarian part. Likewise, Serbia featured universal manhood suffrage from 1888. Besides these three cases, no other country in the region enjoyed this basic institution of liberal democracy.

The experience of WWI, the Bolshevik revolution and its exposition effect on the region, and the national liberation revolutions of 1918–22, not to mention the power of the US example and Wilsonian appeal to "make the world safe for democracy," made

---

14 The only exception was Hungary, where semi-authoritarian order had prevailed since 1921 as a result of successful counter-revolution and resultant repression. As a result, the first fully free elections in modern Hungary took place in 1990. Hungary has a uniquely strong authoritarian tradition.

the old conservative hierarchical order of Eastern Europe untenable. In most countries of the region mobilized masses and their leaders created fairly radical liberal democracies, often dominated by peasant and moderate socialist parties. Challenging pre-existing social hierarchies, the new regimes introduced far-reaching social reforms, including land and property redistribution. Frequently, the logic of nationalism and social egalitarianism reinforced each other—the upper classes and bureaucratic masters were often aliens, to be purged from newly created national states.[15] As evidenced in electoral outcomes in any free elections (there were plenty of unfree or semi-free ones) in the region, the democratic order enjoyed overwhelming popular support. Conversely, in no country did the authoritarian or radical authoritarian right (fascists), or radical authoritarian left (communists) enjoy jointly a majority popular support, unlike, for instance, in Germany during the 1932–33 period. Moreover, the ruling forces of authoritarianism, which mostly took over by the 1930s, were nowhere in Eastern Europe fascism, and had to rely on violence, corruption, and manipulation, not popular support, to sustain themselves in power.

A regional overview, going from north to south, makes the region-wide positive pattern of democratic political development clear, while exposing national variance, setbacks, and complexities of the process.

In the Baltic republics of Latvia and Estonia armed struggles for independence led to the successful establishment of fully democratic states by 1920. Both carried out radical land reforms that amounted to dramatic social revolutions, as both featured very unequal land distribution prior to 1914. Estonia and Latvia sustained liberal democracies until 1934, when authoritarian leaders Konstantin Päts (in Estonia) and Kārlis Ulmanis (in Latvia) took over and suppressed political parties. These included radical nationalist/fascist movements such as Vats in Estonia and Pērkonkrusts in Latvia. In Estonia the regime was liberalizing again by 1938 and return to full

---

15 Remarkably, these features of post-WWI revolutions were not repeated in 1989, where restoration of capitalism and therefore of an unequal economic order was actually the goal. Additionally, the "aliens" were already long gone.

democracy was clearly a possibility when independent Estonia and Latvia were terminated by the Soviet invasions in 1940.

In Lithuania the land reform was carried out with less vigor than in Latvia and Estonia, while nationalism (chiefly anti-Polish, but also anti-Jewish) clearly poisoned the fractious liberal democracy, which succumbed to an authoritarian coup carried out by Antanas Smetona in 1926. His regime was semi-authoritarian, and featured increasing repressiveness in the 1930s. However, in 1938 Smetona was forced to transfer the Memel region to Germany and to open diplomatic relations with Poland. These defeats weakened his regime so much that he was forced to seek political support from the opposition, thus reopening prospects of a return to liberal democracy. This chance was cut short by the Soviet invasion of 1940.

Poland was born as a liberal democracy even more factitious than Lithuania—this comparatively large mini-empire of 32 million people (1931) featured a dramatic proportion of ethnic minorities: chiefly Ukrainians (13.9 percent), Jews (10 percent), Belorussians (3.1 percent), and Germans (2.1 percent), which together amounted to close to one-third of the country's ethnic makeup. Ukrainian and Belorussian populations lived in unified blocks in the eastern part of the country, had national aspirations and actively resisted the Polish rule, while Germans in the western part of the country, supported by their co-nationals in Germany, sought revenge and, later, a total destruction of Poland.

Since Poland was created out of pieces of the German, Russian, and Austro-Hungarian empires, the problem of unifying the country was mind-boggling. Besides the fact of ethnic minorities (each of which was divided into different political factions), the Polish political spectrum was dramatically fragmented as a legacy of past participation into three different sets of political institutions. However, all Polish political forces agreed on the establishment of a liberal democracy, which also instituted far-reaching social reforms, including women's suffrage, a land reform, a universal social and health insurance, and so on. The country's elected parliament included a huge proportion of representation by peasant parties without whose participation no majority parliamentary government was possible. Since the majority of the country's population was rural, its national government was thus a fair reflection of the country's social structure.

The Polish liberal democratic experience in its full-blown form ended in 1926, when the military national hero of the country's struggle for independence Józef Piłsudski took over and established a semi-authoritarian regime of *sanacja* (sanation), which became progressively more repressive until his death in 1935. His lackluster successors continued the regime without Piłudski's legitimacy and charisma. However, the regime never fully suppressed political parties (with the exception of the Communist Party) and free media. While anti-Semitism, authoritarianism, and violence were rife in Polish politics, openly fascist political forces were minuscule and suppressed by the *sanacja* regime during the Piłsudski era. Significantly, in 1938 the regime allowed for free municipal elections, which were won by the opposition. Whether the country could return to liberal democracy was an open question when the country was invaded in 1939, and, then, a huge number of its inhabitants were murdered by the Nazi and Soviet regimes.

Interwar Czechoslovakia stands as a model of functional liberal democracy throughout the entire interwar period, regardless of the country's dramatic diversity, which actually exceeded the Polish one. In this fairly large state of 14.7 million people (1930) the Czechs were barely a majority of 51 percent, while the rest of the population was German (22 percent—over 3 million), Slovak (16 percent), Hungarian (5 percent), and Rusyn (4 percent). The Germans lived in the solid bloc in the western part of the country (Sudetenland), Slovaks occupied the east, with Hungarians concentrated in the southeast and Rusyns in the southeastern Carpathian region. This dramatic pluralism was ably managed by the hegemonic bloc of five moderate mostly Czech political parties (the so-called Pětka), which always won the elections and managed the country through politics of concessions, tolerance, and democratic compromise with the minorities. While no doubt pluralistic and competitive, the Czechoslovak democracy was therefore limited: the Pětka was always in charge, which, compared to the Polish chaos and authoritarianism might well have been the best solution for an Eastern European democracy. Lubricated by a relatively sound developed

## Globalization: Empires and Nationalism

economy, Czechoslovak democracy functioned well until 1938, when German political aggression, and the externally engineered partition of Czechoslovakia, embodied in the infamous Munich Accords, killed the country. In 1939 Czechoslovakia was partitioned between Germany, nominally independent Slovakia, Poland, and a resurgent, vengeful Hungary.

Yugoslavia, or formally the Kingdom of Serbs, Croats, and Slovenes (1918–29, later, the Kingdom of Yugoslavia) was by far the most pluralistic of the new states, with no ethnic majority: this country of 12 million people (1918) was inhabited chiefly by Serbs and Montenegrins (39 percent), Croats (24 percent), Slovenes (8.5 percent), Bosnian Muslims (6 percent), and Macedonians/Bulgarians (5 percent) (Banac 1992, 58). Croats and Serbs clearly dominated the country and the conflict between them defined it: Serbs were divided, but their hegemonic faction tended to be statist centralizers, while Croats were dominated by peasant parties, and demanded liberalism and autonomy. The country featured choppy pluralism constantly on the verge of, or descending into, mass violence, but was managed through mechanisms of parliamentary democracy until 1929,[16] when King Alexander suspended parliamentary government and managed the country under the cover of Yugoslavian unity, which often meant equal-opportunity repression of all nationalist forces—a premonition of communist Yugoslavia. He was assassinated by pro-Bulgarian Macedonian separatists working together with Croatian violent secessionists (the Ustaše, "insurgents") and Italian intelligence services in 1934. The government devolved to Regent Paul, who tried to practice the politics of compromise and return to liberalism. As a result, in 1939 Croat autonomy was proclaimed and Croat leader Vladko Maček became vice prime minister of Yugoslavia. The politics of return to liberalism was cut short as the regent was overthrown by the anti-German Yugoslav military, which put 17-year-old King Peter in charge. Hitler's reaction was a German invasion, division of the country, and the orgy of interethnic violence sponsored and abetted by the

---

16 A good historical analogy to post-2003 Iraq, another country with no ethnic majority, featuring elections and constant violence between constituent nationalities and different factions and parties of the same nationality.

Germans. Whether the country could return to liberal democracy is an open question—clearly, it could exist as a loose confederation of nationalities—but interwar Yugoslavia was destroyed from the outside, not from within.

The fact that Bulgaria emerged from WWI defeated and stripped of disputed border territories was actually beneficial to the country's democratic development, as the nationalistic elites that led the country to the disastrous war were gone and replaced by radical left-wing forces, especially a party representing the country's vast 80 percent peasant majority: the Bulgarian National Agrarian Union (BANU) and its leader Aleksandar Stamboliyski. After winning the parliamentary elections of 1920 against its chief rival, the Bulgarian Communist Party, the BANU formed a government which put Agrarian ideology to work and instituted radical and real economic reforms aimed at improving the fate of the peasants. However, confident in their power, BANU government overreached by 1922, turning increasingly authoritarian, corrupt, and repressive, which pushed oppositional forces together. Since Stamboliyski's resolutely anti-nationalist policies also alienated the country's military and pro-Bulgarian/Macedonian nationalists, the coalition of anti-Agrarian forces, tacitly supported by Bulgarian communists, overthrew him in 1923 and instituted a counter-revolutionary "white terror" government of Alexander Tsankov. A period of savage repression, anti-government violence, and instability followed until 1926, when King Boris III restored political moderation and return to liberalism, culminating in another Agrarian parliamentary victory in 1931. However, the country's dismal economic situation as a result of the Great Depression led to another round of instability, a military coup of 1934, and King Boris III's counter-coup of 1935. The king restored limited liberalism and pluralism, which continued in the relatively stable country even when it allied with Nazi Germany. Liberalism in Bulgaria was finally terminated by a Soviet-directed communist takeover of the country between 1946 and 1947.

Romania was defeated in WWI (in 1917) before it won it in 1918, but the country's elite disastrous performance in the war was for everyone to see. Nevertheless, the country almost doubled

## Globalization: Empires and Nationalism

its territory, mostly at the expense of Hungary (Transylvania), Bulgaria (Dobruja), and Russia (Bessarabia). The resulting "Greater Romania" (*Romania Mare*) included substantial national minorities and gained hostile neighbors, thus assuring the continuation of nationalism and the dominant theme of Romanian politics. Indeed, the country's chief problem, rural poverty and underdevelopment, was not addressed. While free elections and parliamentary government within a framework of constitutional monarchy emerged after 1918, the resulting governments were corrupt and unstable. Initially dominated by the corrupt and clientelistic National Liberal Party, after 1927 the parliamentary government passed into the hands of the moderate and reformist National Peasant Party. However, hopes for liberal democratic political and positive economic development were dashed when the Great Depression devastated Romania, and its politics became more violent and authoritarian. In Eastern Europe it was in Romania (alongside Hungary) that a substantial fascist movement emerged, led by the Christian fundamentalist/ anti-Semitic and ultra-violent Iron Guard and its leader Corneliu Codreanu. However, he was assassinated and his movement repressed by authoritarian King Carol II in 1938, who, in turn, was forced to abdicate and was replaced by the government of Marshall Ion Antonescu in 1940. Antonescu created a governmental coalition with the Iron Guard, only to turn against it in 1941, when he crushed the fascists with Hitler's connivance. The violence, authoritarianism, and fascist prominence in Romanian political life of the interwar period would make the country the weakest of the Eastern European liberal democracies, if not for the special case of Hungary.

Hungary was the only country in the region not to become a liberal democracy in the interwar period. As a result of the savage civil war that followed the Hungarian revolution of 1919, the "white terror" government of Regent Miklós Horthy eventually took power and instituted a semi-authoritarian regime that represented a strange throwback to pre-1914 days. Horthy's Hungary was ruled by a neo-feudal landowning/upper-class elite in charge of a country that featured limited liberalism and parliamentary elections that never really provided for executive turnover in power. Deprived of 72 percent of its pre-war territory, and with 3.3 million

Hungarians living outside the country's borders, the small 8.5 million (1930) Hungary was the revisionist nationalist power *par excellence*, pining for the restoration of its empire and for a failure of post-WWI order. These desires were initially constrained by international treaties and an anti-Hungarian "Little Entente" alliance of Romania, Yugoslavia, and Czechoslovakia, but, with the failure of the Versailles order in the late 1930s and support of Nazi Germany, a remilitarized Hungary struck for glory in 1939–41, regaining most of its pre-war territories at the expense of "Little Entente" countries. The country also featured a substantial fascist movement, chiefly embodied by the Arrow Cross Party. The fascists were partially repressed and partially accommodated by Horthy's regime, whose brand of authoritarian conservatism was at odds with fascism. However, the country never managed to fully extricate itself from an alliance with Nazi Germany, and was defeated as an Axis power, subject to Soviet occupation, and, after a period of limited pluralism in 1945–47, to a full communist dictatorship. It is not an exaggeration to state that the first free elections in Hungarian history took place in 1990, such was the strength of authoritarian tradition in Hungary.

In conclusion, the stereotype of interwar Eastern Europe as all authoritarian and radical nationalistic (or worse "fascist") is false. The strength of anti-authoritarian forces across the region varied dramatically from country to country, being the weakest in Hungary and Romania and the strongest in Czechoslovakia. Fascism, contrary to other forms of authoritarianism, was weak, and nowhere really came to power. A possibility of a return to liberalism was strong in many countries at the end of the 1930s: such was definitely the case in Poland, Lithuania, Estonia, Yugoslavia, and Bulgaria. However, the entire liberal global economic order failed, which led to fascism in Germany. This was a result of disastrously short-sighted and non-cooperative Western policies, with the chief culprit being the United States' unilateralism and isolationism.

It was not the authoritarian nationalism of interwar Eastern Europe that decisively destroyed political liberalism and free nation-states in the region. That destruction came externally from Nazi and then Soviet imperialisms. Indeed, if we interpret the strength and survival of political liberalism in the region as a result of ideological globalization, it showed itself in possession of internal resilience despite inhospitable economic (de-globalization, the Great Depression) and political (failure of Versailles order, growing strength of revisionist powers) circumstances. Empires, not nation-states, proved to be the chief enemies of liberalism and globalization in Eastern Europe. Conversely, nations of Eastern Europe, to a large extent, embraced liberal and democratic political cultures, and thus proved themselves desirous of both external and internal freedom, which came with a measure of openness to the world and therefore to globalization.

## Nazi/Fascist Empire, 1930s and 1940s

As I already mentioned, one way to see Hitler's design on Eastern Europe is as a simple continuation of German WWI imperialism, albeit more radical. However, if we adopt our traditional definition of imperialism as an ideology of a single state dominating a large land mass and a large number of people, then, imperialism, by definition, results in a multinational and multicultural hierarchical state that also exerts influence over weaker states. Yet, Hitler was an Austrian German whose obsession was racism and racial purity—he therefore saw his native multinational Habsburg Empire as a negative example of something that the new German Reich should never try to be. Indeed, his ideal of the Third Reich was to be a gigantic homogenous German nation-state incorporating territories of Poland, Ukraine, Belarus, and parts of historical Russia, all stripped of their native inhabitants and settled by the Germans, who, according to Hitler, suffered from a dire shortage of land and resources and lacked the necessary Lebensraum ("life space"). Enslavement of the "natives" could also be a possibility in this new imperial scheme, but it was clearly sub-optimal, as multinationalism of any form threatened the ideal of racial purity. Likewise, the idea of allied nations in the parts of Eastern Europe to be incorporated directly into the Nazi uber-nation-state had to be rejected: an allied Polish statelet or a notion of Ukrainian or Russian puppet states was contrary to Hitler's vision. His was not the German imperialism of

WWI, and not really (even though the Nazis often claimed so) a version of Western European overseas colonialism applied to Eastern Europe.[17] The vision was novel and unprecedented, and its subtext was a deliberate genocide to be applied on a scale unseen in history. This, at least, was the theory.

In practice, the Nazi empire developed in ways that to a large extent directly contradicted the theory. Hitler wanted to create his land empire in Eastern Europe based on an understanding with the British Empire and with the United States that the German continental state did not threaten the Anglo-Saxon powers and did not intend to overthrow their sea-based supremacy. While Great Britain seemed to be playing along with this vision up until the Munich Accords of 1938, the Polish refusal to ally with Germany against the Soviet Union, the British outrage over the Nazi takeover of Czechoslovakia, and joint British-French security guarantees to Poland threw the whole vision out of whack. In some sense, this confirmed another Nazi theory, which is the notion of an international Jewish plot that included the United States, Great Britain, and France (all controlled by "Jewish bankers") in alliance with the Soviet Union (another "Jewish state") to destroy and contain Germany in the name of an international regime of global domination: in Hitler's terms, "Jewish internationalism." Still, this meant that a global war different to the one envisioned by Hitler had to be fought.

As it happened, Hitler's Germany became entangled in a war against Western European powers that stood in the way of German expansion in Eastern Europe. These dynamics brought together the two enemies of the West—Stalin's Soviet Union and Nazi Germany—in a pact to jointly dominate Eastern Europe. Poland

---

17 In memoirs and writings of German theorists and leaders one can find constant colonial metaphors, deliberately or ignorantly stripped of a sense of reality of actual colonialism. For instance, one can find constant references to Germany ruling newly conquered Soviet territories "like the British rule India" with a complete, deliberate, or actual ignorance of the realities of the British system of indirect rule through countless native intermediaries in India. Instead, the Germans often deliberately rejected any form of intermediary native authority, preferring the most brutal form of direct enslavement, and then justified it with false colonial metaphors.

## Globalization: Empires and Nationalism

was crushed and occupied by these two powers. Baltic states were invaded and destroyed by the Soviets, while Germany occupied the Bohemian part of Czechoslovakia as a "protectorate," and created a subject Slovak state. Overwhelming German political and economic influence was also extended over nominally sovereign Hungary, Romania, Bulgaria, and Yugoslavia. When the latter rebelled, it was crushed, occupied, or divided jointly with fascist Italy and revisionist Hungary. While the Soviet Union pressured Romania to give up Bessarabia, Hungary, with German support or directly by force, took back its "lost" parts of Czechoslovakia, Romania, and Yugoslavia.

In the West and Scandinavia, German troops emerged victorious, and Germany, jointly with Italy, found itself dominating all of Europe, with the lonely Great Britain standing in the way of the Third Reich. In other words, instead of a "pure" ethnic empire in Eastern Europe, by mid-1941 Nazi Germany (in alliance with Italy) found itself in possession of a multinational all-European empire, some under direct occupation, but most under indirect rule as a system of associated states in a bewildering variety of circumstances. Hitler also found himself at war with Great Britain, which he had wanted to avoid. Thus, while happy about the success of their military conquests, Nazi rulers stumbled upon a multinational empire of a mind-boggling complexity for which they really had no theory or plan, and at war against Anglo-Saxon powers for which Germany did not prepare (Mazower 2008).[18]

Frustrated with Britain's continuous resistance, and seeing that the United States was mobilizing in support of Britain and would come into a direct clash with Germany sooner or later, Hitler decided that his plan for a German super-nation-state could be implemented, after all, with the invasion, conquest, and ethnic cleansing of the Soviet Union. This would also create a sphere of economic domination sufficiently large enough to defeat the British and counter the tremendous economic and industrial power of the United States. Thus, in June 1941, Nazi Germany invaded its Soviet "friend" and, by November 1942, overran more than half of Soviet

---

18 German naval and strategic bombing/naval air forces were weak or non-existent. Germany's gigantic armament efforts of the 1930s were almost all aimed at a continental land war.

industrial and agricultural potential, reaching to the oil-fields of the Caucasus and inflicting close to four million casualties (dead or prisoners of war [POWs]—most of whom were starved to death) on the Red Army. This was the world's largest single military conflict in history, and Germany almost won it. Germany's Eastern European allies also joined in the conflict; Hungary and Slovakia reluctantly, and Romania enthusiastically.[19] Genocide of Jews, enslavement and mass killing of the local population, and unspeakable brutality accompanied the German and allied conquests. Then, following the November 1942 counter-offensive at the "Battle of Stalingrad" (a succession of giant operations that should be called "a battle for the Caucasus and Southern Russia") the Soviet Union, supported by Western allies, found within itself the material and morale to decisively defeat Germany and its allies on the Eastern Front.

Even before the German military was defeated on the battlefield, the whole German imperial project started failing on its own terms, defeated by its own internal contradictions. The premise on which the whole idea of a gigantic Aryan nation-state rested was, after all, the notion that Germany needed a huge landmass—Lebensraum— to itself, to be settled by pure "Aryan" people. That landmass was indeed acquired in the course of the 1939–42 conquests, but this area needed to be "cleansed" of their native populations, and Germans, supposedly suffering from land scarcity, had to be found to settle these territories. Nothing remotely resembling this mad scheme happened—the natives refused to die or proved impossible to be cleansed even in the territories directly attached to the Reich (mostly ex-Polish), while German settlers for the gigantic colonization schemes in Ukraine, Belarus, and Russia were nowhere to be found. Indeed, desperate to "create" Germans to fight the war or settle territories, the Nazi state found itself at work forcibly or administratively converting the native population of questionable

---

19 Bulgaria refused to declare war on the Soviet Union, but found itself formally at war with Great Britain and the United States. When in 1944 Bulgaria wanted to desperately switch sides in the war, it declared war on Nazi Germany, but even after that, the Soviet Union declared war on Bulgaria and invaded the country. Bulgaria thus found itself at war with Nazi Germany and the Soviet Union at the same time.

## Globalization: Empires and Nationalism

German ancestry into "ethnic Germans" (Volksdeutsche), making a mockery of the whole theory of racial purity. The only "success" of Nazi Germany was thus the Holocaust, a mad mass extermination of Jews, which directly harmed the war effort and became the synonym of modern evil.

Moreover, by 1943, in the grip of total war, Germany found itself desperately short of labor, and so followed the wholesale importation of foreign labor, semi-free or enslaved from all over occupied Europe, directly into the heart of ethnic Germany. By 1945 Germany was more ethnically diverse than ever before or since—it was Nazi Germany, not the postwar Federal Republic of Germany, that created the most "diverse" Germany, and turned the Reich into a country of six million unwilling "gastarbeiters" of every possible nationality. Likewise, the Wehrmacht was so desperately short of soldiers that the army of proud Aryans was increasingly staffed by questionably ethnic Germans or a bewildering variety of non-Germans: former Russian POWs, Ukrainians, Azeris, Western European volunteers, and others. Indeed, most of the "German" divisions that opposed the allied Normandy landings in 1944 were made up of Eastern European "volunteers," while Polish forces allied to the British grew by leaps and bounds by drafting Polish POWs who previously served in the Wehrmacht. The "pure" Aryan empire turned into a parody of itself.

While half of Eastern Europe found itself under direct Nazi occupation, the other half—Slovakia, Hungary, Romania, Bulgaria, and Croatia—became Nazi allies. Relationships between these states and Nazi Germany followed no systematic pattern—as the Nazi political system was one of organized chaos of competing leaders and bureaucracies, a similar chaos was projected into the country's external relations, which were managed bilaterally and *ad hoc*, freely mixing the craziest genocidal racism and stunning pragmatism. This chaos, mixed with brutality, was especially visible in the territories of former Yugoslavia, where Germany (jointly with Italy) created a complex system of domination based on an allied state of Croatia and other subjugated territories. While Croats in their majority welcomed their own state, the Ustaše who were put in charge of it had marginal support in pre-war Croatia. Perhaps because of it, and driven by their own fascist and racist ideology, the Ustaše launched a program of mass genocide of Serbs and Jews in Bosnia and Krajina, which marked a descent of former Yugoslavia into an orgy of multisided war and interethnic violence worse than anything the region had suffered before. Italy and sections of German leadership were appalled by the chaos and the bloodletting, but the massacres were approved by Hitler and ideological Nazis. Similarly, Romanian medieval massacres of Jews in Bessarabia were approved by the Nazis. Not imperialism but nihilism seemed, at times, to be the true underpinning of the Nazi scheme.

On the other hand, there was a pragmatic side to Nazi imperialism, most visible in Western Europe, which Germany dominated "accidentally" and for which the Nazis had no real theory or plan. Dominated by civilian bureaucrats, technocrats, capitalists, and military pragmatists, Germany's plans and policies in the West sometimes appear like a Nazi version of the European Union (EU). In Eastern Europe this dynamic probably most manifested itself in the Protectorate of Bohemia and Moravia. Paradoxically, Hitler hated the Czechs most among the Slavic nations (unsurprising for an Austrian German), and Nazi pronouncements were full of genocidal intentions against the Czech. However, once the Czechs surrendered peacefully, Germany found itself in possession of the tremendously productive agricultural and industrial potential of Bohemia. As its continuous unimpeded operation was crucial for the German war effort and it was manned by largely docile Czechs, the Nazi bloodthirstiness against the Czechs was largely suspended during the war.[20] The region was therefore peaceful until the very end, when Czechs, supported by Russian armed forces created to be German allies, rose in uprising in Prague in May 1945.

By 1944 German defeat was assured, and German allies in Eastern Europe tried to break up the relationship and get out of the war. Slovakia rebelled against the German rule, Romania successfully

20 The one exception was the massacres carried out by Germans after the Acting Reich Protector for Bohemia and Moravia, Reichard Heydrich, was assassinated in 1942. Otherwise, Germans brutally repressed any signs of actual resistance in the Protectorate, but the resistance was weaker than in any other directly occupied country of Eastern Europe.

# Globalization: Empires and Nationalism

switched sides in the war, and Bulgaria, likewise, declared war on Germany. Only the Hungarian effort in this respect was unsuccessful, and both Nazi occupying forces and pro-German Hungarian forces were too strong to pry open the German grip on the country. Everywhere in the region, expect for Yugoslavia and Albania, which were liberated by communist guerrillas, Soviet occupation followed the German one, which brought about another chapter in the region's history.

To conclude and to put the story of the German empire in Eastern Europe in a broader conceptual context: the Nazi episode was a unique example of racist uber-nationalism that unwillingly took on a classical imperial form. The logic of the system was self-consciously an anti-globalization one: Hitler, in his mind, was fighting "Jewish internationalism," so, globalization itself, identified and personified as a Satanic force. The ideology and the system that Nazi Germany created were unprepared to run its multinational empire, and went down to defeat not just because of external blows, but out of its own internal contradictions. In Eastern Europe the system was marked by economic destruction (still, less than the one created by WWI) and mass killings unprecedented in the history of humanity. Out of the rubble emerged another imperial system in the region, the one created by the Soviet Union.

## Communist Empire, 1945–89

Marxism-Leninism-Stalinism (ideology of "communism" or "real socialism") was an ideology in many ways directly opposite to Nazism: instead of a racist uber-nationalism, it preached equality and unity of humanity; instead of anti-globalization, it preached uber-globalization: an eventual disappearance of the state itself and the creation of a global, borderless society was the professed goal of communism. The similarity between communism and Nazism, besides the obvious and superficial one—violent suppression of all opposition and the attempt to create ideologically homogenous societies ("totalitarianism")—was that both were caught in a series of impossible self-contradictions at the core of their project. Nothing illustrates the internal contradictions of communism better than its relationship with imperialism and nationalism, as seen from the vantage point of the Soviet Empire in Eastern Europe. Here there was an essential contradiction between the communist theory and practice.

The relationship between communism and nationalism was complicated. On the one hand, Marxism denied the significance of nations, nationalism, and national differences. For Marx, the key social cleavage was between classes, and "proletarians had no country." On the other hand, Marx and his followers had to recognize the reality of imperialism (and colonialism), national oppression, and cultural/racial differences between people, which were staring them manifestly in the face, and could not simply be ignored. The compromise approach that we see progressively emerging under Marx/Engels, Lenin, and Stalin—the latter a thinker and theorist on the issue in his own right—was as follows: nations and national oppression are real concerns that Marxist-Leninist theory and practice has to recognize and accommodate. However, national oppression, and therefore, animosity between nations is, like all oppression, rooted in capitalism or a system of class oppression in general. Once capitalism and capitalist imperialism are abolished (the primary task—no oppression can be abolished until it happens), the significance of national difference will diminish, provided there is no national oppression. That will happen if national cultures are permitted to "flourish" and nations/ethnic groups are given national autonomy or nominal independence (as socialist countries) to allow for the flourishing. Here was the formula for the creation of autonomous socialist republics (SSRs) in the Soviet Union or nominally independent nation-states in Eastern Europe. The ruling slogan was "national in form, socialist in content." It mattered that socialism was to be preached in Polish and by a nominally sovereign Polish nation-state, provided that the "content" was socialist and a part of a transition towards a borderless and classless—and, in some sense, "nation-less"—global socialist society, in which cultural differences would be stripped of their political connotation, as all oppression was to disappear. Hence, in Eastern Europe the Soviet Union (with the exception of the Baltics, incorporated directly into the Soviet State, as "autonomous republics") supported the continuous

## Globalization: Empires and Nationalism 51

existence of largely post-Versailles nation-states, albeit "socialist in content."

The second key dimension of the Soviet imperial contradiction involved the Marxist-Leninist theory of state. On the one hand, Marx and Lenin preached abolition of the state: the state in the Marxist theory was an apparatus of oppression created by dominant classes to suppress the lower classes, so with no reason to exist once the class oppression was abolished. However, the state still had a reason for a temporary existence when the class struggle was going on—the proletarians needed a state to suppress the bourgeoisie and wage a global struggle for socialism. This temporary state was based on a pragmatic accommodation (in his classic *State and Revolution*, Lenin calls it "a bourgeois state under proletarian control") and could preserve many features of a "traditional" state. If we put the Marxist-Leninist-Stalinist theory of the state and of the nation together, we have a formula for a Marxist-Leninist nation-state, theoretically a contradiction in terms, but justified by its temporality and its transitional nature.

The way in which the Soviet governmental system emerged out of the maelstrom of the Russian revolution and the subsequent Civil War featured a strong, centralized Communist Party in charge of a prioritized and powerful military and security apparatus, which defended "communism in one country" against a hostile capitalist world and, always looming, internal "enemies of the people" who were to be repressed. These enemies, more often than not, were "heretical," real or imaginary, leftists tempting the people to abandon the one and true path set by the party. Another set of enemies were "bourgeois nationalists." Finally, there were "capitalist powers"—Nazi Germany or the United States. To repress these external and internal enemies, the state was all-powerful.

Then, in the Soviet imperial project, the template set by the "communism-in-one country" example of the Soviet Union was copied in all countries of Eastern Europe, whether subjugated by the Soviets as the result of WWII, or communist as a result of internal armed struggles against Axis powers and their indigenous allies (as in Albania and Yugoslavia). Everywhere the same basic system was cloned, with the Communist Party and its centralized apparatus of power, a fair level of militarization of society, a political police in charge of enforcing the party orthodoxy, and subordination of all institutions, at least formally, to the party. The party, in practice, meant a centralized system of power and control formally centered on either the party leader or a nebulous network of a couple of power-brokers in the executive committees of the respective Politburos. The overall design of the system was one of a besieged castle: it created powerfully defended autarkic political and economic states designed for self-protection and an occasional projection of power abroad (Jowitt 1992).

From the Soviet imperial perspective the internal design of communist states posed a challenge: how could countries designed to be "autonomous castles" ever cooperate in a common imperial system? By design, the communist states were geared for conflict and autonomy, not complementarity and cooperation. At the same time, the mythos of a world-wide revolution and Soviet imperial purposes demanded "internationalist unity" of all socialist states, based on the common policy representing the one correct path to the communist utopia. Whose prerogative it was to define the path for all countries of "real socialism" was inherently contestable. How to maintain "socialist unity" in the Soviet Empire became a problem, not just because different subjugated nation-states and their communist leaders often demanded independence, but because the internal institutional design of communist states militated against unity. Indeed, conflict, not cooperation, became the hallmark of communist states in the world: communist Soviet Union vs. communist China, Vietnam vs. Cambodia, Yugoslavia vs. the Soviet bloc in Eastern Europe, and Albania (in alliance with China) vs. the Soviet bloc and Yugoslavia. Communist states were designed for conflict and conflict is what they got.

The whole theory of "national in form, socialist in content" proved to be a sham, based on an illusion that national cultures can somehow be a depoliticized fluff that amounts to national forms of embroidery, dance, or cooking.[21] Socialist nation-states in Eastern Europe, or SSRs in the Soviet Union and Yugoslavia

---

21 Liberalism, another universalist ideology, shares the same illusions with communism.

## Globalization: Empires and Nationalism    53

inevitably practiced nationalism as both form and content of their political life, and in many ways, the half-suppressed nationalisms became more important, not less important, under communism. With formal communist politics becoming a de-politicized and ritualistic mouthing of Marxist-Leninist orthodoxy, national differences between ethnicities and countries became the most important actual content of political life, while Marxism-Leninism was its meaningless form. As a result, the Marxist-Leninist state system emerged as a parody and reversal of what it was supposed to be in theory: instead of a stateless utopia of happy people who put their national differences aside, it became an uber-statist conflictual hell in which national differences took on an increasing significance. The fact that, immediately upon the failure of communism, nations of Eastern Europe seceded from multinational states whenever they could testifies to this reality. Clearly, the reverse of "national merging" and overcoming of national differences happened.

Economic contradictions of "real socialism" and its relationship with capitalist globalization is another key feature of the Soviet Empire of Eastern Europe, which explains its failure and transition back to liberalism and capitalism. In theory, "real socialism" was to be an economic system vastly superior to capitalism, as the selfishness of exploitative upper classes and chaos of the market were to be replaced by an unselfishly motivated pursuit of economic development and growth organized systematically for the common good. At the same time, Marxism-Leninism embraced industrial and technological modernity with a vengeance (in Lenin's famous saying, "Communism is Soviet power plus the electrification of the whole country" (Lenin 1975–9)) and pursued urbanization, industrialization, and social modernization (literacy, etc.) at an accelerated pace. In the context of largely rural, agricultural, and fairly poor societies of Russia and Eastern Europe (there were a few exceptions, such as Bohemia or East Germany), whose economic growth and development were stunted by nearly 30 years of war or crisis (1914–45), the developmental energies of socialism appeared, indeed, prodigious and superior to what the region had experienced under 1918–39 capitalism. Based on the figures reported in the Maddison Project, as of 1950 Eastern Europe nearly doubled its average per capita income as compared to 1930 (from $2,464 to $4,082 in 2011 dollars), and doubled it again by 1970 ($8,241) (Maddison Project 2020). The region had never before experienced as high a rate of growth in per capita incomes—but, significantly, the same and higher pace of growth was later registered in the region under capitalism in the 2000–18 period. However, after the 1970s the growth slowed down to less than 20 percent for the entire decade (from $8,224 to $9,933) and in the 1980s socialist economies hardly grew at all (from $9,933 to $10,344 in per capita income—barely 4 percent for the entire decade). The developmental energies of "real socialism" were thus exhausted by the 1980s, as the system proved itself only capable of a "one-shot" bout of industrialization, growth, and modernization. Unlike in capitalist economies, the stagnation was not cyclical, but systemic and terminal. Thus, instead of being a system vastly superior to capitalism and with boundless developmental potential, socialism proved to be a formula for creating "stuck" shabby urban and industrial economies unable to satisfy Eastern Europe's growing popular clamor for freedom and prosperity. Most importantly, the fact that socialist economies of Eastern Europe were more prosperous than pre-WWII economies no longer satisfied populations that saw the prosperity of the West and had earlier been told that socialism was to be a system superior to capitalism.

In terms of their international economic relations, communist states were caught in several dilemmas. In principle, trade and economic cooperation were to be pursued vigorously among communist states. However, as I mentioned earlier, the statist and autarkic template of the Soviet Union militated against communist economic cooperation, which had to be maintained through administrative rather than market mechanisms and was poisoned by political rivalries. Symptomatic in this respect was the Soviet economic relationship with Romania, which, in the Soviet design for an Eastern European "socialist division of labor," was to be an agricultural and light-industry country. That scheme was completely rejected by Romania's communist leader Gheorghiu Dej, and his successor Nicolae Ceaușescu, who industrialized Romania against Soviet wishes, partially in cooperation with the West and the "dissident" anti-Soviet communist states of Yugoslavia and China.

## Globalization: Empires and Nationalism

This was accompanied by theatrical displays of Romania's political independence from the Soviet Union to the point that Romania's military was geared to repel a Soviet invasion. Some communist countries, such as poor and truculently anti-Soviet and anti-Yugoslavian Albania, pursued policies of economic autarky. Overall, though, trade between socialist countries, with the West, and with the emerging "Global South" grew quite dramatically during the communist period of 1950–73 at an annual compound overage of 9.81 percent, only to fall during the late 1970s and 1980s (Maddison 2006, 127). This last statistic reflects the fact that the entire global economy entered a period of recession, instability, and crises that lasted throughout the 1970s and 1980s.

By the 1970s the communist world was clearly a constituent part of the global economic system which included both the developed capitalist world and the rising "Global South." Generally, the communist relationship with the capitalist world was schizophrenic: on the one hand, capitalism was the hostile realm to be avoided, on the other, capitalist technological modernity was to be embraced. As early as the 1930s Stalin used Western technology, capital, and experts to help industrialize the Soviet Union. The notion was that Western capitalist progress could be raided for its resources and expertise, to help build socialism and thus contribute to capitalism's own demise—as the famous and false (created by Western paranoid anti-communists and falsely attributed to Lenin) saying goes: "capitalists will sell us a rope on which we can hang them." The unexamined flip side of this policy was, what if the act of "buying rope" from capitalists made the communist countries a part of the global economic capitalist system, dependent on the West, while exposing the inferiority of the socialist economic model? This is precisely what happened—the act of "buying capitalist rope" transformed and exposed socialist countries into a clearly inferior and dependent part of the global capitalist economic system, and the process started way before the formal collapse of communism in Eastern Europe. Just like the pre-1918 empires, the Soviet Empire was thus unable to contain forces of globalization from undermining the empire from within—a process that the Soviet Empire itself partially invited.

## 56 Globalization: Empires and Nationalism

Politically, the Soviet Empire in Eastern Europe began with the Soviet forces overrunning most of the region during WWII. The two communist countries that avoided Soviet occupation, Yugoslavia and Albania, established the system with the victory of their own communist guerrillas against weak (Italians in Albania) or chaotic (Yugoslavia) Axis occupations. Significantly, these two countries became enemies of the Soviet Union rather quickly regardless of their ideological affinity to the Soviet system. Also, communist Romania successfully negotiated the withdrawal of the Soviet armed forces in the 1950s and then became a communist country essentially hostile to the rest of the Soviet bloc, regardless of Romania's formal and continuous membership in the institutions of the Warsaw Pact (Soviet-led military alliance organization, equivalent to NATO) and the Council of Mutual Economic Assistance (COMECOM, a Soviet rigid equivalent of the European Community). Thus, communist Eastern Europe included at least three "national communist" countries partially or fully independent of Soviet control.

Following the formula "socialist in content, national in form," the Soviet Union maintained most of the countries of Eastern Europe in the boundaries of the 1930s, which meant a return to Versailles and Trianon, with some modifications. In the north, Baltic countries were destroyed and their territory was directly incorporated into the Soviet Union, as "socialist republics" with formal and nominal cultural and political economy.[22] Poland was stripped of all its eastern territories inhabited by mixed Ukrainian, Belorussian, and Polish populations, but, in exchange, was given ex-German territories in the west and north, from which all the German population was expelled. Given that most Polish Jews were murdered in WWII and the remaining ones emigrated, Poland emerged from WWII as a homogenous Polish ethnic state. Czechoslovakia was restored as a state of Czechs and Slovaks, but stripped of its German population, which just like in Poland, was expelled. In the east, Czechoslovakia lost the Carpathian region mostly inhabited by Rusyns and Hungarians—this was attached to the Soviet Ukraine as "Trans-Carpathian Ukraine." While still multinational,

---

22 This included in the Soviet constitutions the right to secession, which was meaningless until 1990, and, then, exercised with a vengeance.

## Globalization: Empires and Nationalism

Czechoslovakia was much less diverse than before the war. Hungary was simply returned to Trianon boundaries, losing all of its wartime gains. Romania lost Bessarabia (which became Soviet Moldova), but kept Transylvania and the vast majority of Dobruja. Bulgaria, likewise, returned to 1940 boundaries. So did Yugoslavia and Albania, with small adjustments. On balance, post-WWII Eastern Europe featured much more nationally homogenous states than before the war, but multinational Yugoslavia and Czechoslovakia continued to exist, and so did Hungarian minorities in all of the neighboring states—unlike the Germans, the Magyars were not expelled. This reality was important for the post-communist period: with the exception of Yugoslavia, violent nationalism did not return to the region of nominally independent Eastern European states (it did to the former Soviet Union—especially Ukraine).

The general pattern of political development followed by the communist states of Eastern Europe can be divided into three different periods: two very short and a long one. The 1945–48 period was one of limited liberalism and pluralism, when Stalin allowed for states under his control to enjoy a façade of liberal institutions, including semi-free elections, non-communist political parties, and relatively free media, while repressing non-communist political forces under the excuse of "fighting fascism." This façade did not exist in communist Yugoslavia and Albania, where "native" communist regimes were repressive right off the bat, nor in the Baltic republics where post-war Stalinism was especially brutal in suppressing any signs of Baltic nationalism or liberalism.

The second period began in 1948, when harsh Stalinism descended on the entire region accompanied by slavish copying of all and any Soviet institutions. This was followed by repression of any signs of opposition to Sovietism, especially national communist leaders considered insufficiently loyal to the policy of total subjugation to the Soviet "diktat." The Stalinist period ended between 1953 and 1956, that is, between the death of Stalin and the assumption of power by Khrushchev in the Soviet Union. This "transition" to post-Stalinism was accompanied by instability and popular uprisings against Stalinist regimes in East Germany (1953), Poland (1956), and Hungary (1956).

58 **Globalization: Empires and Nationalism**

Finally, the entire period after 1956 until 1989 can be considered a period of slow, halting, and uneven liberalization across the entire Soviet Union and communist Eastern Europe—this was the time when nationalism reasserted itself as a dominant theme of politics in Eastern Europe, and when the countries of Eastern Europe asserted their limited autonomy within the Soviet system. This was also the time when the independent communist mini-empire of Yugoslavia became radically decentralized, and nationalism clearly became the chief pre-occupation of communist politics in Yugoslavia even though open nationalisms were suppressed. During this period communist Albania and Romania, two countries that asserted their autonomy against the Soviet Union, became, paradoxically, more Stalinist in their domestic policies, while Romania opened itself to the world economically.

In countries controlled by the Soviet Union in the 1945–48 period, nationalism was an important source of legitimacy for the new regimes that pretended to be ones of national and social "liberation." After all, all Eastern European countries were new nation-states recently liberated from imperial rule, be it of pre-1918 empires, or of the Nazis. In this last respect the Soviets and their allies seized on the anti-German nationalism, which could be especially exploited as a source of legitimacy for communist regimes in Poland and Czechoslovakia: countries directly occupied by Nazi Germany and with a strong tradition of reciprocated hostility towards Germans. Likewise, anti-German nationalism, coupled to repression of all Yugoslavian nationalisms as the source of Yugoslavia's orgy of killing in WWII, could be a source of legitimacy of Yugoslavian communism, led by charismatic guerrilla leader Josef "Broz" Tito. Even in Hungary, the Communist Party exploited the hatred of Germans and Jews, the latter under the name of a struggle against capitalist exploiters, "parasites," and "speculators." In Romania, suppression of Hungarians and regaining of Transylvania was a subtext of the regime ideology. In Bulgaria, a hostility to the "traditional" enemies—Greece and Turkey—could easily be subsumed by the regime, as both were capitalist countries, and eventually members of NATO. In addition, once Yugoslavia became a "dissident" communist country, Hungary's and Bulgaria's traditional hostility to

## Globalization: Empires and Nationalism

Yugoslavia could easily be exploited by the Soviet Empire. Thus, a subtext of adversarial nationalisms was rife and used by communist regimes across the region, but especially in the 1945–48 and 1956–89 periods.

The nationalism of constituent nations was especially important in the multinational states of Czechoslovakia and Yugoslavia. Following the "national in form, socialist in content" formula, the communist leader of Yugoslavia, Josef "Broz" Tito, formed the country into socialist federal states that included six constituent autonomous republics, each to embody a separate national aspiration: Slovenian, Croat, Bosnian, Serbian, Montenegrin, and Macedonian. Additionally, two autonomous provinces were created within Serbia: Kosovo (to represent the ethnic aspirations of Albanians) and Vojvodina (to represent the multinationality of this area, which included Hungarian, Romanian, and Slovak minorities, besides the Serbian majority). Initially the autonomy of constituent parts of Yugoslavia was of nominal character, but progressively, nationalism seeped into the political life of the country and became the true essence of the internal politics of the Communist Party and state, with Tito manipulating international and interprovincial rivalries in the name of maintaining the state. For instance, Tito repressed the centralist and hardline faction led by a Serb, Aleksandar Ranković, in 1966, only to turn around and repress the liberalizing mass movement of Croats ("Croatian Spring") in 1971. The system could thus be characterized as one of a carefully managed balance of power between nationalities (Ramet 1992) or of universal oppression of all nationalisms in the name of socialist unity. As Tito died, and Yugoslavia liberalized in the 1980s, nationalism only increased in importance, partially as a prop used by authoritarian communist elites, but also seen as a sign of liberation by the masses. Clearly, the 45 years of communism did little to dissolve the force of nationalisms in Yugoslavia—in many ways, mistrust and conflicts between constituent nations were "frozen" rather than resolved.

The Soviet Union destroyed the independent Slovak state (considered "fascist") and restored unified Czechoslovakia. However, the potential for animosity between Czechs and Slovaks, including within the Communist Party, was only subsumed under the façade of unity. Among others, the Soviets themselves could use the national conflict in the name of imperial control of Czechoslovakia. Significantly, the 1968 episode of liberalization and the Soviet invasion of Czechoslovakia was followed by nominal decentralization of Czechoslovakia in 1969 and the creation of nominally autonomous federal Czech and Slovak republics. Just like in Yugoslavia, communism manifestly did little to decisively overcome Czech and Slovak nationalisms and the country was to split peacefully in 1992.

The interlude of high Stalinism between 1948 and 1956 also featured nationalism as a subtext of communist ideology, except the nationalism in question was Russian, and the whole episode represented a throwback to pre-1918 imperialism. In subject countries Stalinism promoted the factions of the respective communist parties most slavishly loyal to Moscow's "Russified" communism, while those communists deemed insufficiently loyal were removed from power, arrested, or executed, mostly for the sin of "right-wing deviationism/nationalism." The rituals of submission also involved a slavish aping of anything and everything of Soviet-Russian provenance, including forms of cultural expression, details of soldiers' uniforms, or institutions. Because the official Soviet culture of the period was a peculiar mix of Russian nationalism and Marxism-Leninism (for instance, the entire Soviet cinema was mostly devoted to celebrating national heroes of pre-communist Russian past, Soviet military uniforms reflect Tsarist era uniforms, etc.) the whole exercise amounted to a form of cultural Russification with a Marxist-Leninist twist, with the latter being reduced to a meaningless ritual and the former being the actual content. Of course, this did not apply to communist Yugoslavia, where the Communist Party created its own forms of communist "internationalist nationalism," tied to Yugoslavia's identification with the non-aligned movement of former Western colonies in the Global South.

The 1953–56 transition from Stalinism across Eastern Europe amounts to rejection of the most abjectly slavish features of Stalinism, including Russification—for instance, the Commander-in-Chief of the Polish military, Marshall Rokossovsky, of a mixed Polish-Russian ancestry, was sent back to Moscow. Countries of

## Globalization: Empires and Nationalism

the Soviet Empire were now allowed to practice (within limits) their cultural, political, and economic autonomy. This included a return to reliance on nationalism to bolster communist legitimacy, which was very pronounced in the cases of Yugoslavia, Albania, and Romania, and took the form of hostility to the Soviet Union and emphasis on indigenous forms of "socialism," which could be fairly liberal (Yugoslavia) or brutally Stalinist (Albania and Romania). In Poland, the regimes of Władysław Gomułka and Edward Gierek practiced their "Polish way to socialism" but allowed for the existence of private agriculture, a fairly liberal cultural politics, and for the existence of an autonomous and insubordinate Catholic Church. Hungary, after a failed national-liberal uprising against Soviet rule in 1956, retreated into limited liberalization of the economy and attempts to create a modern consumer society à la communiste. However, an attempt at a similar liberalization in Czechoslovakia, in 1968, ended up with a Soviet and allied military intervention. In the meantime, Bulgaria remained as the most faithful servant of the Soviets in the Balkans, but its slavishness was also exploited by the country's wily leader, Todor Zhivkov, to gain subsidized goods and markets from the Soviets. Likewise, the East German leaders followed Soviet political orthodoxy slavishly, but created a fairly successful (by communist standards) socialist economy by exploiting the Soviet desire to showcase East Germany as a respectable socialist counterpart to West Germany. Overall, as asserted by the head of the Communist Party of the Soviet Union, Leonid Brezhnev (1966–82) in 1968, no genuine liberalization ("abandonment of socialism") was allowed to occur in the Soviet Empire ("The Brezhnev doctrine").

As already mentioned, the first three decades of communist rule in Eastern Europe were an age of fast economic growth and modernization in the region, which was transformed from mostly rural and agricultural to mostly urban and industrial. However, the growth slowed down later on, as the type of growth that relied on one-time absorption of people and resources into the machine of modernity did not lead to a form of growth driven by innovation and efficiency. The remedy of seeking Western capital and technology to jump-start moribund Eastern European economies also failed. By the late 1970s many countries in the region found themselves in a debt crisis vis-à-vis the West; such was the situation of Poland, Hungary, Romania, and Yugoslavia. History was making a full circle, and Eastern Europe was becoming, again, a part of globalized, Western-led economic modernity. Hammered between insolvable dilemmas of a need for internal legitimacy, economic crisis, militarism, and for Western cooperation to foster the communist countries' economic growth, the Soviet and allied leaders desperately looked for solutions.

The final crisis of communism can be traced to the Polish "Solidarity" crisis of 1980–81, when a massive non-violent revolt of the Polish society forced the Polish Communist Party to first liberalize the country, and then, to massively crackdown on the civil society in December 1981. Supported by the Soviets, the crackdown succeeded initially, but the country's communist government had no long-term solutions to the problems of a deteriorating economy heavily in debt to the West. While the government still used anti-German or even anti-Soviet nationalism ("our crackdown prevented a Soviet intervention that would have been far worse") as a prop to maintain its legitimacy, the communist basis of power was wearing thin. Indeed, all communist countries of Eastern Europe had to face up to the reality that the communist economic model proved to be a developmental dead end. However, the Soviet imperial grip had to relax first, and the impulse from the disintegration of the Soviet Empire had to come from its center.

Under Yuri Andropov, a KGB head who became the General Secretary of the Soviet Communist Party (1982–83) after the death of the senile Leonid Brezhnev, solutions to the Soviet dilemmas were to be found in a neo-Stalinist emphasis on law and order, militarism, and a crackdown on both dissent and corruption, accompanied by relative pragmatism on select economic and political issues. Under the senile Konstantin Chernenko (1983–84), who was terminally ill when ascending to office, the late Brezhenevian orthodoxy and corruption seemingly returned. After Chernenko's death, the ascent of Andropov's protégé Mikhail Gorbachev to the highest office finally marked a full and final attempt to restore dynamism to the decadent system.

## Globalization: Empires and Nationalism

Initially Gorbachev's solutions seemed to follow his mentor's emphasis on law and order and militarism, but this soon led to liberalism, opening to the West, and encouragement of liberalization among the bloc countries. A search for arms-control agreements/ détente with the West and demilitarization was a part of the reform package that soon brought about cuts in military spending and demilitarization of the Warsaw bloc countries. By 1988–89 Poland and Hungary were in full turn towards liberalization, encouraged by Moscow. By the end of 1989, through either peaceful negotiated transitions in Poland and Hungary, or massive upheavals from below accompanied by internal collapses of the regime in Czechoslovakia and East Germany, the communist regimes in East Central Europe ended. This was encouraged by Moscow through an explicit repudiation of Brezhnev doctrine and its replacement by the jokingly formulated "Sinatra doctrine." In Romania, though, Ceauşescu was overthrown by an internal revolt in December 1989 supported by the Hungarian minority, the military, and sections of the popular masses, and, most likely, a Soviet covert operation approved by the West, with his secret police bitterly and bloodily supporting the regime to the end. Shortly thereafter, Yugoslavia disintegrated into constituent parts, and soon descended into a vicious and bloody civil war. In Albania, finally, there was a protracted process of transition that ended up with the Communist Party losing power in 1992. By 1997, however, the country disintegrated into chaos and civil war, which Albania's weak and corrupt state was unable to contain. Stability was only restored through an international United Nations (UN)-authorized armed intervention featuring some ten thousand soldiers.

"Interrupted development" and "return to diversity" is one popular framework for looking at the Nazi and Communist experience in Eastern Europe, as the region can be seen returning to its pre-1939 patterns of development and political boundaries in 1989. However, neither the region nor the world into which it was returning were the same in 1989. For one, Eastern communist countries were transformed into a specific form of non-capitalist urban and industrial societies, and their domestic and international integration into the global capitalist system was to pose unprecedented challenges from within. Second, the world into which Eastern Europe reintegrated after 1989 was dramatically globalized and institutionalized in forms very different from the 1918–39 world. Partially, the lessons of the interwar period were now fully learned, and the West was united with the full participation of the United States. However, that world was to enter into a new period of crises and challenges after 2001, often in connection with the broader interactions with the "Global South." These challenges, in interaction with domestic political forces of Eastern Europe, sparked a renewal of anti-Western and anti-globalization forms of populism and nationalism in Eastern Europe after 2010. This, however, was the second wave of post-communist nationalism. The first wave immediately followed the revolutions of 1989 and took liberal or anti-liberal forms, with an infinite variety of in-between permutations. Clearly, while forces of imperialism and globalization ebbed and flowed in Eastern Europe, different forms of nationalism remained the persistent reality of Eastern Europe.

## Post-communist Expressions of Nationalism after 1989

Liberal nationalism was the subtext of the entire process of the collapse of communism, which, for the publics in question, was conceived as a rejection of an alien ideology and foreign domination. The latter was definitely the case for all of the non-Russian Soviet bloc members and seceding republics of the Soviet Union, where the collapse of the Soviet Empire was celebrated as an opportunity to exercise true national self-determination in terms of both domestic political order and international sovereignty. In Yugoslavia, the constituent nations asserted their sovereignty against a domestic order perceived as repressive of them all. As attempts to restructure the state on a confederal and liberal basis crumbled, a long nightmare of "wars of Yugoslavian succession" followed.

Significantly, in the ambiguous cases of "national communist" in Albania and Romania, the transition to post-communism was also more abstruse and longer than in other countries of the region. In Albania, ousting of the ruling party was not accomplished until

## Globalization: Empires and Nationalism

1992, only to be followed by an internal collapse of the state in 1997 and restoration of order through a foreign intervention. In Romania the collapse of communism was a murky and violent affair, which featured a genuine popular upheaval from below, elements of a military coup/mutiny, and an ambiguous foreign interference. What followed was the hegemonic rule of a former communist apparatchik Ion Iliescu, who at the head of the Social Democratic Party, dominated Romanian politics until 2004, creating a system that did not feature a clean break with the communist past. Even more ambiguous was the special case of the ex-Soviet Socialist Republic of Moldova, which became independent with the collapse of the Soviet Union in 1991, and immediately had to confront an ethno-secessionist conflict in the breakaway region of Transnistria.

In the "normal" cases of post-communist transformation, which included all of the Northern Tier of Warsaw Treaty Organization members—East Germany, Poland, Czechoslovakia, Hungary, the Baltic Republics, and Bulgaria—nationalism was a subtext of the process that sought to create liberal polities featuring free elections, free markets, and civil rights and liberties. Since the break from communism in all these countries avoided major outbreaks of organized violence, and the countries faced no clear prospects of an armed aggression or conflict, the liberal imperative was also attached to an assertive anti-militaristic and anti-nationalist political ideological streak, typical of the aftermath all liberal revolutions. This was especially the case, since communism featured extreme forms of militaristic power politics and exploited nationalisms, which the ideology of anti-communist dissent identified as a part of a "global coalition of aggressive imbecility," or warmongering militarism, East and West (Konrad 1984, 217). Rejection of militarism and violence was universal and with this came suspicion of military institutions, alliances, and preparations for war. As just exemplified by the largely bloodless collapse of the Soviet Empire, the power of ideas and "human spirit" was considered superior to the material power of coercion (Havel and Keane 1985, 21). A most significant expression of this spirit was perhaps the peaceful split of Czechoslovakia in 1992—one of the few cases of an amicable ethnic secession in history.

Liberal politics were confronted with a devastating reality and seeming superiority of nationalistic militarism in the former Yugoslavia. After a decade-long process of institutional decay in the 1980s, and a failure of efforts to negotiate the country's transition into a loose liberal-democratic confederation in the first half of 1991, the country's formal breakup began on June 25, 1991, when Slovenia and Croatia proclaimed independence. The Yugoslav federal military (Yugoslav People's Army—*Jugoslovenska Narodna Armija*, JNA) was the one institution of the failing state with a pre-existing will, plan, and means to coercively resist the breakup. Accordingly, JNA 5th Military District troops attempted a muddily conceived massive show of force by deploying to key strategic points of Slovenia to intimidate the secessionists. Faced with determined and well-planned asymmetric armed resistance of Slovene Territorial Forces (*Teritorialna Obramba Republike Slovenije*, TORS) the JNA actions failed miserably during a "Ten Day War" between June 27 and July 7, 1991.

The Slovenian War of Independence, which claimed around 70 dead and 200 wounded, was just an opening salvo for a series of "wars of Yugoslavian succession," which were waged in Croatia (mostly in the second half of 1991 and then in mid-1995), then in Bosnia (1992–95), Kosovo (1996–2000, mostly in 1999), and Macedonia (2001). By the end of the horror, these wars killed around 140,000 people, most of them in Bosnia, many of them civilians executed as part of a Serbian campaign of mass killings against Bosniaks (Bosnian Muslims). The wars also generated around two million refugees and two million internally displaced people, most of them, again, from Bosnia. All of this amounted to the largest armed conflict in Europe since WWII, at least until the Ukrainian war of 2022. While incomparable to the earlier European conflicts, or to the wars occurring simultaneously in the Global South, the wars of Yugoslavian succession were a sobering reminder of the importance of militaristic nationalism and of weakness of liberal institutions and norms in the world. Especially, the impotence of Western European countries and of international institutions that missed firm elements of military power and political resolve, such as the EC/EU and the UN, was dramatically and serially exposed in

## Globalization: Empires and Nationalism

the course of mostly futile and byzantine diplomatic negotiations and peacekeeping operations meant to create peace and compromise solutions to the conflicts.

Conversely, a naked military force settled the Yugoslavian conflicts. Decisive armed confrontations occurred in 1994–95. First, Croat military forces, superbly re-organized and armed after their humiliating defeat by JNA/Serbian troops in 1991, crushed the Serbs in Krajina in a series of fast mechanized offensives: operations "Flash" and "Storm," the largest military operations in Europe between 1945 and 2022. Then, in 1995 the combined Croat and Bosniak forces systematically defeated and pushed back Bosnian Serbs, who were also selectively bombed by NATO and were forced to accept a compromise peace offered in Dayton Accords in November 1995. Finally, in the spring of 1999, a Serbian counter-insurgency campaign against Kosovo Albanians was stopped by the Albanian guerrilla force of the Kosovo Liberation Army backed by a massive NATO air campaign. What followed was a negotiated Serb withdrawal from Kosovo and a deployment of heavy NATO/Kosovo Force (KFOR) troops in Kosovo in the summer of 1999, leading to eventual Kosovo independence in 2008. In all cases, the "NATO" operations were decisively led, manned, and equipped by the United States. Only in the 2001 case of the armed revolt of Macedonia Albanians against the government led by Macedonia's Slavic majority, did the EU-sponsored negotiations and attempts at a compromise peace seem to have been of importance, eventually leading to a political settlement and an uneasy cessation of hostilities. However, even in this case, the ability of the Macedonian government, supported and partially armed by Bulgaria, to mount a vigorous military response to the insurgency forced the Albanian fighters to a negotiated solution. Realism, not liberalism, seemed to celebrate a triumph as a framework for understanding the former Yugoslavia, but interaction between nationalism, liberalism, and globalization clearly shaped the entire region in the immediate post-communist era.

There were two nations in the former Yugoslavia that sought to revise the pre-existing administrative borders: Serbs, who had a huge presence in Croatia and Bosnia, and Albanians, present as a large majority in the province of Kosovo in the Republic of Serbia, and as a large minority in Macedonia. Both nations were mobilized and fought to either establish their own states and/or national unity or recognition against the other nations: the Serbs battled again Croats in Croatia and against Bosniaks (Bosnian Muslims) and Croats in Bosnia-Herzegovina; while Albanians fought against Serbs in Kosovo and against Slavic Macedonians in Macedonia. Both Serbs and Albanians failed in their project of national unification, but succeeded in carving out their own states or autonomous entities: a sovereign Kosovo for Albanians, and Republika Srpska as an autonomous constituent unit of the Bosnian Confederation in Bosnia. The one nationalist project that completely failed was the one of Serbs in Croatia, in the region of Krajina. Their incipient state was destroyed in the course of Croat military operations in 1995, and the Serbs were forcibly removed or fled from Krajina. The last, bloodless, act of Yugoslavian fragmentation was a secession of Montenegro from the Republic of Serbia and Montenegro in 2006. Thus, out of six constituent republics of communist Yugoslavia, seven states emerged, all based on pre-existing administrative boundaries: Slovenia, Croatia, Bosnia and Herzegovina, Serbia, Montenegro, Kosovo, and Macedonia.

# Chapter 3

# LIBERALISM AND ANTI-LIBERALISM

## *JACEK LUBECKI*

## The Spread of Liberalism and Its Discontentment

As mentioned earlier, communism in Eastern Europe was far from isolated from the global economy and was, in many ways, integrated into the global economic system. However, the domestic political and economic order of communist states was *sui generis*, and it lasted for generations, creating persistent structural and cultural realities. Moreover, regardless of the relatively high economic growth that Eastern Europe experienced during the initial years of communism, the developmental gap between Eastern and Western Europe only increased in the 1945–90 period, mostly due to the slow growth that Eastern Europe experienced in the 1970s and 1980s (Maddison Project 2020).[1] The gap was only to grow in the 1990s, as the costs of transition from a communist economic and social system to liberalism and capitalism proved to be dramatically high in post-communist Eastern Europe.

The global context into which Eastern Europe was being integrated was a part of the problem. By the 1990s the global economy featured highly institutionalized forms of capitalism, which, in the post-WWII West, went through two phases of development: the high-growth "golden age" of 1945–73 post-war recovery, and the crisis/neo-liberal recovery phase from 1973 to the 1990s. Eastern Europe's transition happened during the second phase, when the West dominated global (the International Monetary Fund [IMF], the World Bank, etc.) and

---

1 The average annual per capita income growth in Western Europe during the 1973-90 period was 1.9 percent, as compared to the East European 0.5 percent (Maddison 2006, 160). The ratio of Eastern European per capita GDP as compared to the Western European one decreased from 0.46 in 1950 to 0.34 in 1990 (Persson 2010, 199).

regional (the European Community/European Union, European Bank for Reconstruction and Development, etc.) economic institutions, and settled on a model of capitalist economic development that emphasized macro-economic stability and free markets at the expense of state intervention and concern for full employment. This model, sometimes dubbed "The Washington consensus," was promoted universally in the former communist countries. Additionally, in Western Europe, the drive for monetary unity accompanying the creation of the European Union (EU) in 1992 and introduction of the Euro in 1999 added an extra concern for European fiscal stability. Overall, Eastern European countries were told that they needed fiscal restraints, price stability, open markets, and privatization—the "neo-liberal" model of capitalism—as the secret for economic growth and therefore development. Since many of these countries were in debt, the formal economic machinery of the IMF and an army of Western advisors also supervised the transformation. However, it would be untrue to say that the policies were imposed, as they were also voluntarily adopted and supported by domestic elites of post-communist countries, which could also use the West as the scapegoat for harsh adjustment policies. Thus, both the domestic and international forces were in consensus that the social and economic costs of transformation were worth the price, which was tremendous. The idea was to introduce the decisive package of reforms all at once and quickly: "the shock therapy" model probably first tried in Poland in 1990. The alternative was gradualism, which had some support inside and outside the region. In practice, all countries tried a different mix of gradualism and shock therapy, but in a bewildering variety of permutations.

Aggregate figures show that the 1990s were a "lost decade" for Eastern Europe in terms of annual average per capita economic growth—between 1990 and 1998 the average per capita income in the region grew annually by 0.06 percent, that is, not at all (Maddison 2006, 156).[2] However, this overall figure hides a dramatic

---

2 This does not include former Soviet republics—the Baltic countries, Ukraine, and Belorus—which would make the balance strongly negative (Maddison 2006). Ukraine, especially, experienced the worst economic decline of all post-communist countries, losing close to 80 percent of its overall and per capita GDP.

chronological and country-to-country variability. Essentially, all of the post-communist economies declined in the early 1990s to recover later, but the recovery was at dramatically different rates in different countries (see Table 3.1).

As we can see, three groups of countries took a brutal beating in terms of their economic performance during the 1990s:

1. Countries of former Yugoslavia, with the exception of Slovenia.
2. Former Soviet Republics, except for Estonia and Latvia.
3. Balkan countries outside of Yugoslavia: Bulgaria and Romania. Strangely, Albania performed relatively well.

**Table 3.1** Average economic per capita growth, 1990–98.

| Countries | Average per capita growth rate (%) | % total change in GDP (1990–98) |
| --- | --- | --- |
| Albania | −0.41 | −3.28 |
| Bulgaria | −2.36 | −18.88 |
| Czech Republic | −0.36 | −2.88 |
| Slovakia | −0.01 | −0.08 |
| Hungary | 0.05 | 0.40 |
| Poland | 3.41 | 27.28 |
| Romania | −2.45 | −19.60 |
| Former Yugoslavia (Serbia and Montenegro) | −3.45 | −27.60 |
| Croatia | −1.93 | −15.44 |
| Slovenia | 1.09 | 8.72 |
| Other former Yugoslavia (Bosnia and Macedonia) | −6.37 | −50.96 |
| Estonia | −0.73 | −5.84 |
| Latvia | −0.58 | −4.64 |
| Lithuania | −4.55 | −36.40 |
| Ukraine | −10.24 | −81.92 |
| Belarus | −3.71 | −29.68 |
| Average | −2.04 | |
| Average excluding Belarus and Ukraine | −1.33 | |
| Average excluding all former Soviet Union members | 0.06 | |

War or its absence obviously explains the former Yugoslavia, including Slovenia, where combat lasted ten days, compared to Bosnia, where close to half the gross domestic product (GDP) was lost in the multi-year armed conflict. The variance in overall dramatic economic decline of most of the former Soviet Union also has clear reasons: in most of Ukraine and Belarus communism lasted 70 years, and left behind dramatic cultural and structural legacies, contrary to Baltic countries, where it lasted just half of this period.[3] The largely negative economic performance of Bulgaria and Romania can be seen as a reflection of the countries' pre- and post-communist political legacies that I will illuminate below. Finally, the paradox of Albania's relatively small decline has an obvious explanation: saddled with the wackiest Stalinist dictatorship in Europe until 1991, Albania was the poorest country in Europe and had no way to go but up.

Among the good performers, Poland stood out stunningly, as a country that started its economic recovery as early as 1992, and was growing at an accelerated pace before 2000. Slovakia and Hungary mostly recovered their bearings by the end of the decade, and the Czech Republic reversed its initial negative economic growth. Tiny Slovenia was actually the best performer after Poland: it was by far the richest and most liberalized country of the former Yugoslavia, and the only one to largely avoid armed conflicts during the 1991–2001 decade. All these countries, plus the Baltic countries, tried some version of the "shock therapy" and in all cases this approach seemed to have been vindicated. However, the trauma of transformation also had a delayed and "hidden" cost.

The social cost of transition to capitalism in former communist countries is a separate and often under-appreciated drama. The transition from a non-capitalist to capitalist society in Europe, including in Eastern Europe in the past, took hundreds of years: it involved the dismantling of paternalistic and oppressive institutions, such as serfdom; the creation of individualist private property; and a slow spread of market mechanisms as the determinant of prices. This gradual process was still wrenching and sparked much opposition to capitalism (Engels 2009; Polanyi 2001). In the non-Western

---

3 In this respect, the poor performance of Lithuania is a puzzle.

world, imposition of institutions of modern capitalism on non-capitalist societies often resulted in mass death, not just as a direct result of mass killing, but indirectly, as populations were deprived of their protective institutions and/or lost any sense of social meaning (Shkilnyk 1985; Davis 2001). A similar process occurred in Eastern Europe in the 1990s as the entire social and economic framework of the pre-existing non-capitalist system, including its social certitudes, was dismantled overnight. All of the post-communist societies, including the heavily subsidized former East Germany, experienced a wave of mass premature deaths, especially of middle-aged men, typically due to coronary diseases, cirrhosis of the liver (alcoholism), suicide, and homicide—all indicators of societies and individuals that lost their social bearings. Simultaneously, birth rates plummeted, as did marriage rates, while rates of illegitimacy and abortion (the latter already high under socialism) increased dramatically (Eberstadt 1994, 2010). With estimates of total premature deaths in Eastern Europe during the 1990s varying from three to four million total, and a similar but worse phenomenon in Russia responsible for some six million premature deaths, this amounted to the worst demographic catastrophe suffered by modern societies outside of wars and famine. While the mortality statistics were to eventually improve dramatically in Eastern Europe, and to show definite signs of progress and development in the 2000s, to this day, post-socialist societies tend to have the worst demographic growth indicators in the world in terms of birth rates.

Given how wrenching the economic and social transformation was in post-communist countries, one wonders how post-communist countries managed to transition at all to a period of positive growth and developmental improvement in the 2000s, and did so while being (with the exception of Belarus) at least nominally liberal democracies. One decisive factor was ideological: a widespread public consensus on the desirability of the liberal-democratic model of development felt by the people in post-communist countries. While there were some initial dreams that ex-communist countries would pursue some type of "third way" model of development, they were very quickly discarded in favor of the tested Western model. In this respect, the desire to join the "West" found its natural expression in a desire to join the key European and North Atlantic security and economic institutions: the North Atlantic Treaty Organization (NATO) and the EU. In countries where this feeling was at the forefront—in Poland, the Czech Republic, and Hungary, the Baltic countries, and Slovenia—the respective polities had the least problems infinding a domestic consensus on the desired model of development, and they also recovered economically the fastest from the slump brought about by transition. Conversely, Slovakia, Ukraine, Belarus, Moldova, Romania, Bulgaria, all the countries of the former Yugoslavia with the exception of Slovenia, and Albania all experienced volatile and choppy processes of political transition, and slower economic recovery in the long term (Havrylyshyn et al. 2016). However, there was also a variance within these two groups, and, by various measures, all post-communist countries can be seen as part of a continuum ranging from the best to the worst economic performers.

How to explain the variance among post-communist countries became an object of a dramatic debate in the relevant literature, but the competing explanations can also be seen as complementing each other. From a structuralist perspective, it is easy to point out that the best performers tended to be countries that were the most economically developed ones in pre-communist times (the Czech Republic, Baltics countries, parts of Poland, Slovenia, Croatia, Hungary) and continued to be the richest communist countries. Conversely, the least-developed countries performed the poorest. Historical institutionalists, culturalists, and "civilization" thinkers like Samuel Huntington, in turn, could point out that most poor performers were previously under Ottoman domination or were Christian Orthodox countries, compared to high performers with Catholic or Protestant heritage and previously belonging to the Austrian part of the Habsburg Empire or to Germany. Of course, some countries, like the Baltics and Slovakia, fell in between these different legacies.

If, instead of sweeping logics of culturalism or structuralism, we focus on the empirical realm of different domestic policy formation processes, we find the most compelling proximate factors that explain divergences between different post-communist countries in

## Liberalism and Anti-Liberalism

their processes of finding consensus, or lack thereof, in their search for capitalist development. These factors can be briefly conceptualized as a dialectic between forces of conservatism: either nationalist, neo-communist, or both versus pro-Western, pro-liberal forces that sought a quick integration into Western institutions. The process thus was the quickest where communism collapsed most thoroughly, leaving few strong political remnants capable of resistance against the forces of Westernization: East Germany and Czechoslovakia (Czech Republic), Latvia, and Estonia were the crown examples in this respect. Where ex-communists reformed and became, essentially, pro-Western and pro-capitalist forces (Poland, Hungary, Slovenia, and Lithuania) the will to reform economies and societies and join NATO/EU was equally strong. However, where politically powerful ex-communists were openly hostile to the West and its developmental model (Bulgaria, Serbia) or initially sabotaged the reforms (Romania), the situation was different. Moldova, where ex-communist forces and public opinion remained dramatically divided on economic reforms or prospects of membership in Western institutions, illustrates the pattern vividly. Albania, where the domestic popular will and reconstructed state after 1997 were strongly pro-Western, shows that the patterns of economic and political reform and their relative success does not necessarily have to follow levels of political and economic development. Finally, the countries of former Yugoslavia follow the general pattern, with the caveat that each of them has had to face special considerations flowing from their varying legacies of the war of Yugoslavian succession, and different levels of political and economic development. Thus, where ex-communist forces that easily "recycled" into nationalists were strongest, as in Serbia, the old anti-developmental syndrome of authoritarian nationalist militarism, so characteristic of all Balkan countries of the nineteenth and twentieth centuries, simply continued.

The above analysis also shows that the popular (in Eastern Europe) mythologies of a "clean break" from communism and "return to the pre-communist past" were misguided. Everywhere in the post-communist countries communism created powerful legacies and everywhere ex-communist political forces enjoyed substantial popular support. Even in the Czech Republic and East Germany ex-communists proud of their past enjoyed up to 20 percent of the popular vote in free elections. In Poland, Hungary, and Lithuania recycled ex-communists claiming to be "social-democrats" won popular elections and were hegemonic political forces in the 1990s and into the early twenty-first century, while leading their countries to democracy, capitalism, and Western institutions. Conversely, corrupt, reactionary, or nationalist ex-communists sabotaged or delayed successful transitions in Croatia, Romania, Bulgaria, Moldova, and Serbia. However, in these latter cases these forces often did not oppose liberalism openly but by stealth, hiding behind liberal or generic nationalist slogans, or supposed "social-democratic" ideologies. An open right-wing anti-liberalism was too much against the *Zeitgeist* of post-communism of the 1990s, while preaching a straight return to communism was out of the question.

The one exception, and, in retrospect, the premonition of the future, was Vladimir Mečiar and his regime in Slovakia. As a head of the Movement for Democratic Slovakia (*Hnutie za demokratické Slovensko*, HZDS) he gained power in 1992, solidified it by his party victory in the 1994 parliamentary elections, and ruled the country in an increasingly autocratic style until 1998. He and his party ideology freely mixed left- and right-wing ideologies—welfarism, nationalism, and anti-Western anti-liberalism—in a potent mix that mesmerized the Slovak public. His anti-Hungarian nationalism had a potent appeal in a country that still featured a Hungarian minority, while his anti-Western messages captured a dramatic following in a public brutalized by market reforms. At the same time, Mečiar had solid anti-communist credentials and was a competent politician, able to construct his party-state machine by a mix of corruption and patronage in ways that presaged the post-communist "mafia-states" of post-2010 Viktor Orbán in Hungary and the post-2015 Law and Justice Party in Poland (Magyar 2016). While the dramatic effort of the anti-HZDS parties, united in an anti-Mečiar opposition movement and supported by the West, prevented him from returning to power in 1998, his party actually won the 1998 elections by gaining the plurality of votes. Nationalist-populist politicians similar to Mečiar were to come to power after 2010 in

## Successes of Liberalism and Persistence of Anti-liberalism

Slovakia and elsewhere, when the *Zeitgeist* became friendlier to an open right-wing anti-liberalism.

## Successes of Liberalism and Persistence of Anti-liberalism

The early 2000s were an ambiguous time in the history of Eastern Europe. On the one hand, liberalism and capitalism celebrated their triumphs and historical vindication. Denying the predictions of naysayers and pessimists, economic growth finally returned to all of the post-communist world, including Russia, and the pace of economic growth was spectacular—the fastest ever experienced by the region. Based on Maddison Project data the entire region (including Russia) more than doubled its per capita GDP between 2000 and 2010 as it moved from $8,983 in 2000 to $17,044 and continued growing, albeit at a much-decelerated pace until 2020. As all countries in the region experienced economic growth and development, most also joined Western economic and political institutions: by 2020, most Eastern European countries were members of NATO and the EU, the exceptions being Belarus, Ukraine, North Macedonia, Moldova, Serbia, Bosnia, and Kosovo—with Albania and Montenegro being members of NATO but not the EU, and all countries of Europe with the exception of Belarus being at various stages of candidacy to the EU.

The economic and integrative progress of the region was accompanied by its globalization. Perhaps unsurprisingly, out of 45 countries (which include all major economies) examined in the world by the Bertelsmann Stiftung in 2020, the top 8 countries with the highest percentage increase in the globalization index between 1990 and 2018 were all Eastern European; from the top: Romania, Slovenia, Bulgaria, Lithuania, Poland, Latvia, Estonia, and Slovakia. In the same index, Hungary was 14th, the Czech Republic was 23rd, and Russia 25th (Sachs et al. 2020a, 2020b). Eastern European countries' relative gains from their globalization, as compared to their 1990 per capita GDP, were also the highest in the world: out of 15 countries that registered the highest globalization-induced growth in per capita GDP in the world (with number 1 being China) 9 were Eastern European. On the total globalization index for 45 countries, Eastern European countries found themselves from 12th position (Czech Republic) to 31st (Romania), all ahead of such countries as Israel, Japan, Turkey, and South Korea, and only behind Western European countries (Sachs et al. 2020b). Arguably, no countries in the world, with the exception of China, Chile, South Korea, Ireland, Portugal, Greece, and Turkey globalized as quickly and successfully as Eastern Europe between 1990 and 2018.

The success of development in Eastern Europe also translated into social welfare trends that reversed and undid the brutal indicators of the early 1990s—from the middle of the 1990s all social indicators improved across Eastern Europe, at different rates, which roughly tracked the progress of economic development across the region (Brainerd 2010). By 2010 Eastern Europe was catching up with Western Europe across all categories of social, political, and economic development. That was in contrast to most of the former Soviet Union, where, with the exception of Baltic countries, authoritarianism ruled and socioeconomic development was erratic or non-existent (Brainerd 2010).

Still, and regardless of the success of liberalism and globalization, anti-liberal and anti-globalization forces persisted in Eastern Europe, and in the 2010s were given a second lease on life. Several trends contributed to that, and some had to do with the very success of Eastern European transformation. For one, integration of Eastern Europe into Western institutions meant that the region was now exposed to global conflicts and forces involving the West: the 2001–20 "war on terror" and the Middle Eastern crisis, resulting in the 2011–19 wave of refugees were some of such trends, and these crises are described in the chapters that follow. Second, the very developmental success of Eastern Europe meant that political concerns of Eastern Europeans were becoming similar to the West, which meant the spread of anti-immigration populist nationalism—a Western phenomenon—into Eastern Europe. Third, and similar to the 1930s, the crisis of globalization at its Western core, starting with the Great Recession of 2007–12, shocked the entire world and continued reverberating in Eastern Europe until 2020–22, when

COVID-19 and escalation of the Ukrainian crisis added a new layer of crises to the old ones.

As mentioned earlier in the narrative, the opposition to liberalism in Eastern Europe prior to 2010, and certainly prior to 2000, centered on neo-communist forces that often embraced full-on nationalism, an easy transition given how much crypto-nationalism was already embedded in communist politics. This happened, for instance, in the former Yugoslavia, where both chief protagonists of the drama, Slobodan Milošević of Serbia and Franjo Tuđman of Croatia, were former communist officials. Some of the opposition took a "stealth" form in which liberalism was nominally embraced in theory but sabotaged in practice, as was the case with Ion Iliescu's "social-democratic" regime and party in Romania. Right-wing populist anti-liberalism was fairly rare and marginalized. For instance, the anti-Semitic Hungarian-revisionist antics of István Csurka gained him the support of 5 percent of Hungarians at the peak of his popularity in the mid-to-late 1990s. The nationalist Catholic-fundamentalist and populist League of Polish Families gained 8 percent of the Polish vote in the national parliamentary elections of 2005, only to fall to insignificance in the 2007 elections. Its Polish left-wing populist counter-part (a relative rarity in Eastern Europe) "Self-Defense of the Polish Republic" party of Andrzej Lepper gained 11.4 percent of the Polish vote in 2005, only to dwindle to 1.5 percent of the vote in 2007 and disappear from the scene. Similarly, the Greater Romania Party (*Partidul România Mare*, PRM) peaked in the Romanian parliamentary elections of 2000 with 19.48 percent of vote, only to see its support cut down to 3.16 percent in 2008. All these parties peaked by the time the Great Recession struck Eastern Europe in 2008–10.

Because of its tight economic and financial integration with the West, Eastern Europe as a whole was especially vulnerable to the economic shock of the Great Recession of 2008, and its results lasted in the region until 2015. Especially hard hit were the Baltic countries and Hungary, which had to impose financial austerity measures as the cost of economic aid from the IMF and the EU. However, the reaction of the two could not be more different: while the Baltic countries stayed the course of financial and economic integration with the West, the cost of the Hungarian recession and austerity in 2010 was an overwhelming electoral victory for Viktor Orbán's Fidesz (in Hungarian, Fidesz—*Magyar Polgári Szövetség*, Hungarian Civic Alliance) party with its nationalist-populist message and program. In the meantime, Poland weathered the Great Recession splendidly, continuing its spectacular economic growth under the leadership of the Civic Platform (in Polish, PO—*Platforma Obywatelska*) centrist party of Donald Tusk. It was only in 2015, and under no specific economic pressure, that the PO party narrowly lost the elections to the right-wing populist nationalist Law and Justice (in Polish, PiS—*Prawo i Sprawiedliwość*) party, and its allies united in a fragile "United Rights" electoral alliance led by Jarosław Kaczyński. Other Eastern European countries suffered different rates of economic contraction, accompanied by the rise, to varying degrees, of nationalist populism. However, there is no one-to-one correlation between economic and political variables in the region. Rather, countries followed their own political paths as defined by their political cultures, institutions, and contingencies. An overview of the strength of anti-liberal parties in the region shows that political cultures, geopolitics, and national antagonisms, rather than socioeconomic variables, define the relative strengths of anti-liberal political forces in the region (see Table 3.2).

From Table 3.2 one can clearly see the overwhelming strength of anti-liberal parties in the countries where raw nationalism, based on past intra-regional conflicts or resentment against the "West," is simmering most strongly. This is definitely the case in parts of the former Yugoslavia: Serbia, Bosnia, North Macedonia, Kosovo, Montenegro, and in Romania and Hungary, countries with their own authoritarian legacies and nationalist conflicts. Conversely, anti-liberalism is weakest in the Baltic countries and, at least nominally, in a mono-national country reconstructed under Western tutelage: Albania. Poland, Bulgaria, Croatia, the Czech Republic, Moldova, and Slovenia fall into the middle category. No doubt, anti-liberal forces are strong across the region except for the Baltic countries. How do we explain the general trend and the variance from the long-term perspective of our book?

**Table 3.2** Relative strength of anti-liberalism in Eastern Europe, 2010–22.

| Rank order | Countries | Strongest populist-nationalist/anti-systemic/neo-communist/systemic corruption parties | Elections | Percentage of votes of the leading populist party | Peak showing all anti-liberal parties' vote added |
|---|---|---|---|---|---|
| 1 | Serbia | Serbian Progressive Party (SNS) (centrist-populist)-led coalition | 2020 | 63.02 | 80.55 |
| 2 | Federation of Bosnia and Herzegovina (Bosnia) | Party of Democratic Action (nationalist Bosniak Muslim party) | 2014 | 27.87 | 78.38 |
| 3 | Republika Srpska (Bosnia) | Alliance of Independent Social Democrats | 2014 | 32.67 | 78.38 |
| 4 | North Macedonia | VMRO-DPMNE (nationalist, right-alternative to Social Democratic Union of Macedonia) | 2016 | 39.39 | 77.26 |

*(Continued)*

**Table 3.2** Continued

| 5 | Romania | Social Liberal Union (alliance of Social Democratic and National Liberal parties) | 2012 | 58.63 | 73.87 |
|---|---|---|---|---|---|
| 6 | Hungary | Fidesz-KDNP | 2010 | 52.73 | 69.4 |
| 7 | Montenegro | Democratic Party of Socialists of Montenegro | 2020 | 35.06 | 67.61 |
| 8 | Kosovo | Vetëvendosje (vaguely nationalist catch-all left-wing party) | 2021 | 50.28 | 67.29 |
| 9 | Slovakia | Direction—Social Democracy (Robert Fico's party) | 2016 | 28.28 | 51.59 |
| 10 | Poland | Law and Justice | 2019 | 43.59 | 50.4 |
| 11 | Bulgaria | GERB-SDS | 2014 | 32.67 | 50.03 |
| 12 | Croatia | HDZ-HSLS-HDS-HDSSB | 2020 | 37.26 | 48.15 |
| 13 | Czech Republic | ANO (Action of Dissatisfied Citizens), a centrist populist party | 2017 | 29.64 | 48.05 |

| 14 | Moldova | Party of Socialists | 2019 | 31.15 | 46.17 |
|---|---|---|---|---|---|
| 15 | Slovenia | Slovenian Democratic Party | 2014 | 34.49 | 36.69 |
| 16 | Lithuania | Labour party (personalistic, "centrist" party of Viktor Uspaskich), in gov. 2012–16 | 2012 | 19.82 | 19.82 |
| 17 | Estonia | Conservative People's Party of Estonia | 2019 | 17.76 | 17.76 |
| 18 | Latvia | For a Humane Latvia | 2018 | 14.25 | 14.25 |
| 19 | Albania | Party for Justice, Integration and Unity | 2017 | 4.81 | 4.81 |

Note: Data compiled from electoral reports. For each country, the data reflects the peak combined performance of nationalist-populist, neo-communist, corrupt, and anti-liberal parties.

## Liberalism and Anti-Liberalism

Disaggregating and analyzing the term "anti-liberal parties," which I aggregated for simplicity in Table 3.2, is an important part of the explanation. More often than not, in their majority and when in power, they represent long-standing and deeply rooted political forces in the respective nations, which adapted to the illiberal political environment of their countries, but also shaped this environment from the very beginning of post-communist transformation. If populism in the West/Western Europe is defined by its grass-roots rebellion and anti-establishment nature (like in the classical cases of the *Front National* in France or *Lega Nord* and its permutations in Italy), the term is largely a misnomer for Eastern Europe, where the ruling anti-liberal parties have been the establishment, or, at least, the alternative establishment to pro-Western liberal centrist forces for a while. Eastern European anti-liberalism is thus closer to Trumpism in the United States, inasmuch as Trumpism is a "from above" adaptation—led by a freelancing and opportunistic political entrepreneur—of a long-standing established party to a changing political environment. Moreover, as many observers of Trumpism, like Stuart Stevens in his *It Was All a Lie*, rightly noticed, Trumpism represents a culmination of a long-standing populist trend of the Republican party, in evidence since at least the 1970s (Stevens 2020). A term that we would like to suggest for the dominant forms of anti-liberalism in Eastern Europe and the United States is "popularism." Denoting a "from above" form of political praxis, it uses the appeal of nationalist populism to effect a takeover of a modern liberal-democratic nation-state by a pre-existing section of the political elite seeking to engineer forms of electoral appeal and state institutions that result in a monocratic political order and the elimination of effective political opposition.

An overview of the anti-liberal political forces and their rule in Eastern Europe from their strongest to their weakest forms will illuminate the current political shape of the region.

In Serbia, the dominant Serbian Progressive Party (*Srpska napredna stranka*, SNS) is actually a splitter party from the ultra-nationalist Serbian Radical Party (*Srpska radikalna stranka*, SRS) of Vojislav Šešelj. Under the leadership of Tomislav Nikolić and Aleksandar Vučić the SNS has been the dominant party of Serbia

## Liberalism and Anti-Liberalism

since 2012, replacing the successor (ex-communist) Serbian Socialist Party (*Socijalistička partija Srbije*, SPS) of Milošević and Dačić, which ruled the country in the 1990s. Both the SNS and SPS have been characterized as "nationalist," "populist," and "pragmatic," the former with a presumably right-wing ideology and desire to integrate Serbia into the EU, while the latter has been presumably left-wing, but evolved in ways similar to its rival. Both parties have also been accused of violations of liberal and democratic norms, and capturing the state through corruption, patronage, and illiberal electoral practices: a syndrome of what Magyar correctly calls "the mafia state" but misinterprets as unique to Hungary (Magyar 2016). Indeed, the "mafia-state" syndrome seems to be dominant in Eastern Europe.

In Bosnia, both of its components, the Federation of Bosnia and Herzegovina, and the Republika Srpska, are dominated by their respective nationalist parties: the Party of Democratic Action (*Stranka demokratske akcije*, SDA) representing Bosniaks (Bosnian Muslims), the Croatian Democratic Union of Bosnia and Herzegovina (*Hrvatska demokratska zajednica Bosne i Hercegovine*, HDZ BiH) representing Bosnian Croats, and the Alliance of Independent Social Democrats (*Savez nezavisnih socijaldemokrata*, SNDS) representing the Serbs. The former two parties are simply long-standing hegemonic nationalist parties of their respective communities, capable of a fair degree of corruption and illiberal politics, and indifferent to anything but their nationalist advocacy. The latter party was supposed to be a pragmatic, liberal, and pro-Western alternative to the original Bosnian Serbs' radical nationalist party, the Serbian Democratic Party (*Srpska demokratska stranka*, SDS), but significantly the SNDS evolved in an anti-liberal direction, following the inevitable logic of electoral adaptation to conditions of raw and simmering nationalist conflict. Neither of the dominant Bosnian parties are particularly "populist," as contrary to the nationalists, they resemble nothing more than the ruling Balkan parties of the 1920s and 1930s where nationalism served as a universal language of politics, covering social hierarchies and corruption in the name of national unity necessary to fight against the "others" (the West, the Serbs, Croats, Muslims) who are presumably responsible

**Liberalism and Anti-Liberalism**

for all evils. As it is, as of 2021 Bosnia-Herzegovina, together with Albania, is the most corrupt country of Eastern Europe: to find more corrupt ones, one has to visit Russia or Ukraine.

The politics of North Macedonia is a constant back-and-forth between two parties: the Internal Macedonian Revolutionary Organization—Democratic Party for Macedonian National Unity (*Vnatreshna makendonska revolutsonera organiztsya—Demokratska partiya za Makedonsko Edinstvo*, VMRO-DPMNE) and the Social Democratic Union of Macedonia (*Socijaldemokratski Sojuz na Makedonija*, SDSM). The former presents itself as "Christian democratic" and "pragmatic" but features virulently nationalist leaders and anti-liberal programmatic components, freely mixing them with monumental corruption and patronage whenever it comes to power. The latter is admittedly "social-democratic," a more liberal and presumably less corrupt alternative to VMRO-DPMNE, representing the former (reformed) ruling communist party of Macedonia. However, while the SDSM government has led North Macedonia since 2016 protests (dubbed "the colorful revolution") overthrew the corrupt rule of VMRO-DPMNE, corruption in North Macedonia only increased between 2016 and 2021, as based on Transparency International ratings for the country (Dimitrievska 2021).

In Romania, the Social Democratic Party (*Partidul Social Democrat*, PSD) represents the continuation of the corrupt "left-wing" "party of power" of Ion Iliescu, which ruled the country in the 1990s, whereas the National Liberal Party (*Partidul Național Liberal*, PNL) presents itself as a catch-all right-wing alternative to PSD, and, fittingly, as a successor of a Romanian 1875–1947 party of the same name. The parties' oppositional nature did not prevent them from coming together in a grand coalition in 2012, when their power peaked. Otherwise, though, the parties compete against each other, and this competition and the pressures of the EU led to the country's improved corruption rating between 2014 and 2021. In Eastern Europe, Romania's Transparency International corruption ratings are similar to Hungary's and Bulgaria's, and way better than those of Serbia, North Macedonia, Bosnia, Moldova, and Albania for that matter (see Table 3.3). Indeed, Romania's relatively

## Liberalism and Anti-Liberalism

**Table 3.3** Eastern European and neighboring countries on Transparency International Index, 2021.

| Countries | Global rank (from best to worst) | Score (higher is better) |
| --- | --- | --- |
| Estonia | 13 | 74 |
| Lithuania | 34 | 61 |
| Latvia | 36 | 59 |
| Slovenia | 41 | 57 |
| Poland | 42 | 56 |
| Czech Republic | 49 | 54 |
| Slovakia | 56 | 52 |
| Croatia | 63 | 47 |
| Montenegro | 64 | 46 |
| Romania | 66 | 45 |
| Hungary | 73 | 43 |
| Bulgaria | 78 | 42 |
| Belarus | 82 | 41 |
| Kosovo | 87 | 39 |
| North Macedonia | 87 | 39 |
| Serbia | 96 | 38 |
| Moldova | 105 | 36 |
| Albania | 110 | 35 |
| Bosnia and Herzegovina | 110 | 35 |
| Ukraine | 122 | 32 |
| Russia (for a comparison) | 136 | 29 |

Source: Transparency International Corruption Perception Index, 2021, https://www.transparency.org/en/cpi/2021

high position in the rankings in Table 3.2 might be an artifact of PNL pairing with the definitely anti-liberal/corrupt PSD in the 2012 elections—if the two parties are considered separately, and PNL is not considered anti-liberal, Romania's position in the anti-liberalism rankings much improves.

The cases of Hungary, Poland, Slovenia, and Croatia are very similar: in all cases the currently ruling nationalist-populist parties represent long-standing malleable political forces, which adapted to their political environment. In Poland, the Kaczyński brothers' party *Porozumienie Centrum* (Center Agreement) was a pragmatic, centrist, and liberal party that was crucial in the formation of the first freely elected Polish post-communist party government in the 1991–92 period. After several permutations, which involved a stint in power as a part of the governing coalition between 1997 and 2001, the Kaczyński brothers' political organizations formed the Law and Justice Party (*Prawo i Sprawiedliwość*, PiS) which won the elections of 2005 and formed a government together with the Self-Defense and League of Polish Families parties between 2005 and 2007. Regardless of its alliance with populists, the PiS still presented itself as a pragmatic liberal center-right party, and its chief achievement of the 2005–7 period was lowering taxes on businesses. Only in 2015 did the PiS begin to win elections as a populist-nationalist party with an openly anti-liberal agenda and program, which, moreover, paid off electorally—the party won the 2015 and 2019 parliamentary elections, and the 2020 presidential elections. Significantly, though, the party's control over national government stands on a single deputy in the national parliament (as of 2022), and its victory in the 2020 presidential elections was secured by a difference of 1.35 percent of the popular vote.

Similarly to the Kaczyński brothers and PiS, Viktor Orbán and his Fidesz-KDNP party alliance (*Fiatal Demokraták Szövetsége—Kereszténydemokrata Néppárt*, Alliance of Young Democrats—Christian Democratic People's Party, Fidesz-KDNP) in Hungary represent one of the oldest political forces in post-communist Hungary. Fidesz was formed as early as 1988 and was the governing right-center and liberal party in power between 1998 and 2002. Only after the electoral alliance with KDNP in 2006 and during the parliamentary election of 2010 did Fidesz-KNDP adopt a program of building "illiberal democracy," which, like in the Polish case but more so, paid handsomely in terms of electoral support, as the party overwhelmingly won the parliamentary elections of 2004, 2008, and 2022. With few exceptions, the party monopolized the politics of provincial Hungary—with Budapest remaining an opposition stronghold—and it clearly appeals to the "deep country" with its anti-Western and anti-liberal resentments, and traditional social values that freely mix post-communist

# Liberalism and Anti-Liberalism

89

egalitarianism with nationalism, xenophobia, and social-cultural traditionalism.

The dominant party of Croatia, the Croatian Democratic Union (*Hrvatska demokratska zajednica*, HDZ), is the nationalist "party of power," which came to power even before the country became independent and ruled Croatia in the 1990s under Franjo Tuđman. The party lost power a couple of times, but remained the dominant force and has been in power since 2016 evolving in a more pragmatic and liberal direction and leading the country to membership in the European Union. The HDZ still includes strongly nationalist factions.

Likewise, in Slovenia, the dominant Slovenian Democratic Party (*Slovenska demokratska stranka*, SDS) has been variously in and out of power since the 1990s and only recently (June 1, 2022) lost power to the competing Freedom Movement party of Robert Golob. The party and its charismatic, authoritarian leader, Janez Janša, have a definitely nationalist-populist nature, but do not seem to have achieved the level of domination attained by its Croat and Hungarian counterparts.

In Bulgaria, GERB (*Gradhzani za evropesko razvite na Bulgaria*, Citizens for European Development of Bulgaria), led by the charismatic and corrupt Boyko Borisov, is the leading nationalist populist party. In this case, the force he represents is relatively new politically as it came to power in 2009, but Borisov and his party ruled the country, with a short interruption between 2013and 2014, until 2021. Monumental corruption and ties to organized crime did not prevent GERB from being tremendously popular at the poll, using a classical mix of populist slogans, nationalism, pragmatism, and patronage. Significantly, GERB and Borisov lost the elections of 2021 to another populist party, called "There Is Such a People," led by a TV personality Slavi Trifonov.

While in Poland, Hungary, Croatia, and Bulgaria dominant "popularism" is represented by presumably right-wing political forces, in Slovakia, Moldova, Kosovo, the Czech Republic, Lithuania, and Montenegro populist forces take either "centrist" or left-wing guises. The classical example is the Direction—Social Democracy (*Smer— Slovenská sociálna demokracia*) party of Robert Fico, which freely mixes extreme nationalism, socialist welfarism, anti-Western and anti-liberal slogans, and corruption and patronage when in power. Fico and his party mostly ruled Slovakia between 2006 and 2020, with the party's popularity peaking in the 2012 parliamentary elections, at 44.12 percent of the popular vote, but the party has been out of power since 2020.

Why have the Baltic countries largely avoided the dominance of "popularism"? All the ingredients for the syndrome are manifestly there, including an acute nationalist conflict, given the presence of the Russian minority, and difficult, bumpy economic transitions compounded by the severity of the economic crisis in the 2008–12 period. Geopolitical considerations seem to be at work here: for the tiny vulnerable Baltic countries, securing Western support and membership in Western institutions through sterling and unquestionable liberal credentials and practices seems to be the best defense of their national interests. Thus, paradoxically, realism, in this case, leads to liberalism. The Baltics are not unique in that syndrome. The existence of a liberal democratic Mongolia, a country sandwiched between non-liberal giants, China and Russia, is difficult to explain without the role of geopolitics and the need to secure Western support through sterling liberal credentials. The fact that the Baltics are relatively wealthy and have a strong liberal tradition certainly helps.

Finally, how do we explain Albania, where, on the face of it, openly illiberal political parties are hardly present, but which is the second most corrupt (after Bosnia-Herzegovina) and poorest (after Moldova) country in Europe? Clearly, institutional mimicry and "imperial adaptation" are at work, as all mainstream political forces in Albania do their best to maintain a liberal façade to secure continuous Western aid and approval. In many ways, one is reminded of Albania under the Ottoman Empire, where the Ottomanized Albanian elite participated in the government of Istanbul and its outward modernization and Westernization of the nineteenth and twentieth centuries, while the "deep country" led its un-modernized and medieval life irrespective of the elite. The analogy has its limits: Albania's deep country is certainly participating in the processes of Westernization, globalization, and modernization today, but the contrast between the country's liberal façade and deeply illiberal reality remains.

## Conclusion: Eastern Europe between Nationalism and Globalization

The overall success of post-communist Westernization and globalization in Eastern Europe in developmental and economic terms is a fact. The prevalence of anti-liberal democratic politics in the region is also a fact, which lends itself to various interpretations. Inasmuch as populism (or "popularism" in the United States) is prevailing and a growing facet of Western and perhaps global (see the rise of Modi in India) politics, Eastern European politics can also be seen as a sign of "success" of globalization and Westernization— after all, the region is reflecting global political patterns. However, a deeper analysis of forms of political life in Eastern Europe shows that behind the façade of novelty, the dominant anti-liberal political forces of the region hide long-existing political elites and the prevailing theme of nationalism. This should not be surprising in the region defined by nationalism over the last two centuries, and where countries barely regained independence from direct forms of imperial control thirty years ago.

Inasmuch as Western globalization of the late twentieth and early twenty-first centuries takes highly institutionalized forms, for many Eastern Europeans the coming of global capitalism and institutions such as the EU appears as a new form of imperial control or "colonization." The fact that these institutionalized forms owe a lot to the lessons of 1914–39 when the global order was blown to pieces and violent illiberal forces were unleashed, seems often to be lost on Eastern Europeans pushing against "colonization." For Orbán, presiding over a Hungary still resentful over Trianon, pushing the world back to pre-1914 realities might be a deliberate venture, even though one wonders why anyone would want a return to a world that so obviously self-destroyed.

However, if the lessons of 1914–39 are to truly be applied to today's situation, it is not Eastern Europe that can generate the destruction of global order—at the most, it can be a catalyst for such an act of self-destruction that would have to be generated from within the global Western core. Regardless of the prevalence of anti-liberal political forces in Eastern Europe, liberal-democratic institutions and capitalist development continue in the region, and continue to generate a pushback against the most virulent forms of anti-liberalism. Only with the center of liberal globalization, the West, imploding from within can one expect a destruction of liberal order across the world and in Eastern Europe. Nothing would generate this type of implosion faster than the United States returning to nationalist isolationism, like it seemed to be doing under President Trump in the 2016–20 period. Likewise, a victory of virulently anti-EU forces in any major Western country of continental Europe can generate a similar implosion. The possibility of such an implosion casts a long dark shadow over the future of the region.

# Chapter 4

# ETHNIC CHALLENGES FROM WITHIN AND WITHOUT

*JAMES W. PETERSON*

## Ethnic Warfare and Conflict within the States

The nationalist factor had historically been a double-edged sword within the region of Eastern Europe, and it continued to be in the entire post–Cold War era. After President Wilson, at the end of WWI, issued his "Fourteen Points" with their heavy reliance on the principle of national self-determination of nations, the question immediately emerged of what constituted a "nation." For example, was it the brand-new Czechoslovakia or was it each of the principal ethnic groups within that state? Touchstones for analysis of this conundrum include the wars in Bosnia-Herzegovina in 1992–95 and in Kosovo in 1999, the near civil war in Macedonia at the turn of the century, the role of Russian minorities in each of the northern Baltic states after their achievement of independence, the role of the long-standing Turkish minority in Bulgaria, and the perplexing situation of the Transdniestrian Russians within Moldova. Three of the theoretical perspectives utilized in this book can cast light on these challenging and abiding scenarios. Legacy Theory is enlightening, for it highlights the historical roots, in some cases over a lengthy time frame, of these ethnic conflicts. Divergence Theory helps to explain why so much tension and even actual war has emerged due to the sharp cultural differences among these groups. Clearly, in each of these settings there is also a challenge to Public Management for state leaders who wrestle with the dilemma of how to mold the ethnic differences and tensions into a workable whole that would make their state effective and viable within the region.

## Presence of Russian Minorities in Estonia, Latvia, Lithuania

One vital ethnic issue with looming regional security significance is the presence of important Russian minorities in the three Baltic states of Estonia, Latvia, and Lithuania. Many of those citizens are in those countries due to Russianization decisions that were characteristic of Soviet times. Moscow encouraged or compelled their movement into the Baltics in order to dilute the non-Russian character of those republics so that there would be a better fit for them in the Soviet Union. Achievement of that Russian aim was difficult, for the three republics had significant experiences with autonomy prior to 1940, and their own cultures and languages were very different from that existing in Russia. Given their small size and proximity to Russia, it was no surprise that, as new states, they all pushed for membership in the North Atlantic Treaty Organization (NATO) and the European Union (EU) early in post-communist times. The two alliances were more than willing to bring them in, for their level of economic and educational development had traditionally been the highest in the USSR! In spite of their new-found independence and membership in the Western alliances, their small size and location continued to enhance the sense of threat from the immense cloud of next-door Russia. Both Estonia and Latvia shared a border with the enormous Slavic state to the east, while Lithuania co-existed with the Russian exclave of Kaliningrad lodged between their territory and that of Poland. Whenever the West stirred up Russian concerns, such as during the heated debate over the American plan for a Missile Defense Shield in 2008–9, based in Poland and the Czech Republic, the Moscow response was inevitably an announcement that a military build-up in that exclave might be forthcoming. Following the Russian takeover of Crimea in 2014, Baltic concerns came to the surface, and NATO put a much higher priority on their requests while re-locating considerably more personnel to that region that also included Poland. If that move was decisive, parallel concerns about the Baltic future escalated through the roof after the Russian invasion of Ukraine in February 2022. Central to all of these concerns was the huge worry

# Ethnic Challenges Within and Without

that Russia would exploit the Russian minorities in these three states in ways that might undermine their security or even question their existence.

Estonian nationalism emerged with force in 2007 when they removed a bronze statue of a WWII Russian soldier from their capital city of Tallinn and transferred it to a cemetery outside the city. Russia reacted in support of both their own WWII contributions and members of the Russian minority in Estonia by threatening to cut off oil supplies (Peterson 2011, 152–53).

Russian ethnic nationalism in the Baltic states also played a role in the politics of Latvia when the leadership of the state imposed Latvian education and language restrictions on their Russian minority (Michta 2006, 75–82). Further, they required that ethnic Russian teachers in their country deliver all their classes in the Latvian language. If a Russian in Latvia wanted to become a citizen of their state, it was necessary to pass successfully tests on the Latvian language and history (O'Flynn 2005, 45). Discussions between Russia and Latvia also took place in order to finalize post–Cold War borders. The result was a trade-off in which Latvia gave up the Pskov Oblast in 2007, in order to keep Russian oil flowing in from its company Transneft. That company had threatened to cut off oil to Latvia earlier in 2003 (Europe 2003, 42).

In Lithuania, 16.5 percent of its population was Russian, but the state closed down the only Russian TV network in 2007. The Russian exclave of Kaliningrad became a thorny issue between Russia and Lithuania as well. The exclave was actually located between Poland and Lithuania, and so Russians who wanted to go from there back to Russia had to deal with Lithuanian restrictions (Michta 2006, 75–82). Since Lithuania had by then joined the EU, they had to follow their rules for such transit and thereby required that Russian citizens interested in such travel needed visas to make such a trip (White and Light 2007, 459).

In sum, Russian ethnic nationalism made its voice clear in the reactions against Baltic restrictions in Estonia, Latvia, Lithuania, and their exclave in Kaliningrad.

## Bosnian War, 1992–95

The worst of the Balkan Wars of the early 1990s was the one centered in Bosnia-Herzegovina for a full three years. No ethnic group possessed a majority in the population in this country that had existed for decades as a republic in Yugoslavia. However, the Albanians/Muslims were the largest group, the Serbs second in size, and Croatians a distant third. The local Serbian military attempted to push Muslims and Croats back into smaller territorial holdings, and eventually the newly shaped country of Yugoslavia, dominated by Serbia, invaded as well to create a strong military force that was able to further push the other two groups back and out of much of their traditional geographic areas. This military effort raised memories of their view in previous years that Yugoslavia was in reality a Serbian-dominated state rather than a federation of co-equal minority groups. In 1995, the discovery of the mass grave of Muslims at Srebrenica pulled at the Western conscience to the extent that NATO carried out air strikes on Serbian positions. The result was a Serbian retreat and the convening, under the leadership of President Bill Clinton, of the Dayton Meeting and resulting Dayton Agreement. A tricameral Presidency of Bosnia-Herzegovina was a key result and it preserved the Chair position for a Muslim who represented the largest ethnic group in the state. NATO occupation and management created some stability in conjunction with the new set of local leaders, but the EU replaced the Western military alliance in that role in December 2004. That unique partnership preserved peace and stability, but in the setting of the COVID-19 virus crisis, there were questions about the future of that tricameral solution in 2022.

The devastating war in Bosnia-Herzegovina was a direct consequence of powerful and conflicting ethnic-nationalist forces. The population consisted of a 43 percent Muslim plurality, a 33 percent Serbian population, and a smaller 10 percent Croatian group. The country of Croatia had a strong interest in the fate of its brothers and sisters in Bosnia, but they ended up becoming part of a Croat-Muslim Federation in 1993, and that made some sense in light of their relatively small numbers. After the commencement of Bosnian Serb military moves against the Muslims in that state, outside Serbian

## Ethnic Challenges Within and Without

troops from the old Yugoslavia intervened ostensibly on behalf of the creation of a Greater Serbia. In fact, their Yugoslav People's Army (JNA) took control of the Bosnian Serb forces and also supplied equipment and weapons with the result that Serbs eventually got control of 70 percent of Bosnian territory, a figure well beyond their 33 percent share of the local population (Roskin 2002, 169–70; Csergo 2008, 97). The eventual conflict among those three nationalities in Bosnia resulted in 200,000–300,000 wartime deaths, with a likely 8,000 of them at the Srebrenica massacre in 1995. This result occurred with the presence of 26,000 United Nations Protection Force (UNPROFOR) troops on the ground and also efforts of their Dutch contingent to stop the forced exit of Muslims to their place of death (Baskin and Pickering 2008, 290). These human outcomes constituted an incredibly high price and sacrifice so shortly after the announced Western expectation that such tragedies were not possible in the post–Cold War world.

As a delayed response, NATO carried out a twelve-day military operation called Deliberate Force. The result was such pressure on the Bosnian Serbs that they were willing to go to the Dayton peace conference and sign the Dayton Agreement. That agreement stipulated a reduction in Serb-controlled territory from 70 percent to 49 percent, still considerably above their percentage of the population in the country. Territorial decisions attempted to satisfy the three nationalities whose conflicts had caused the war. One unit was Serb and the other was a Bosnian-Croat Federation. In case conflict should break out again, a follow-up agreement two years later gave the High Commissioner of the UN the power to override Bosnian governing institutions (Baskin and Pickering 2008, 291). In that way, international control continued after the NATO operation in an attempt to prevent such massive suffering again in the future. In addition to political administration through the UN, NATO continued to maintain order through military management under the heading of the Implementation Force (IFOR), and soon its replacement, the Stabilisation Force (SFOR). In order to include an important factor of local neighborhood responsibility for the military presence and exercises of outsiders, there was a concerted effort to include military forces from Eastern European states in the Bosnian peacemaking effort. Slovakia sent 600 advisors, while Bulgaria positioned a transport platoon in the state from 1998 to 2001. Early contributors to the Western alliance military operation included Slovenia, Romania, Hungary, and Latvia. In December 2004, the EU created a peacemaking force called EUFOR, and that unit took over management from NATO, although the military alliance continued to provide the needed military equipment. The presence of East European troops continued on to the point that all ten new NATO members had made contributions by the end of 2005 (Peterson 2011, 65–66). Clearly, the military involvement of nearby Eastern European states was preferable to the exclusive engagement of the countries from the western part of Europe as well as Canada and the United States. The latter set of nations had the military power to bring about the Serb withdrawal and reduced role in Bosnia. However, their distance at a geographic and overall development level would have been more off-putting to the population of those who made up the total population of Bosnia-Herzegovina. There was a greater identification with the similar struggles through which the fellow Eastern European states had gone, both under communism and through the immediate post-communist period. Their common experiences in that sense created more empathy for the Balkan states that had struggled so greatly in the latter period.

### *Kosovo Conflict with Serbia, 1999*

The conflict between Kosovo and Serbia was on the surface similar to the struggles between Serb and non-Serb ethnic groups in Bosnia. However, the circumstances were profoundly different. Whereas the Serbs had gone across national borders in 1992 into a country, Bosnia, that was no longer part of their Yugoslav Federation, the movement into Kosovo in 1998 entailed an effort to control a section of their own shrunken Yugoslav state that was 90 percent Albanian. This made NATO involvement in the struggle more questionable and challenging. The military alliance would have been moving into a civil war rather than attempting to help a state defend itself. The force of nationalism thus bore a two-sided framework, for Serbia wanted to preserve the Yugoslav state in its existing

## Ethnic Challenges Within and Without

form while Kosovo dreamed eventually of declaring a nation-state of its own, and that dream became a reality in 2008.

War between the two nationalities consumed the entirety of the year 2008, and many reports of Serb atrocities against the Kosovars came to the surface in different ways. Therefore, in the fall of the year, the UN Security Council issued Resolution 1199 that condemned those excesses and their large humanitarian price tag. In 1999 the parties to the conflict took part in the Rambouillet Conference in an effort to prevent the use of outside military force. President Clinton took the lead in managing a NATO air attack on Serbian positions, and that was successful in getting the Serbian President, Slobodan Milošević, to pull most Serbian troops out of their Kosovo Republic. The NATO aerial bombing campaign received the name Operation Allied Force (OAF) and there was no ground campaign by its troops due to the urgent need to avoid accusations that they violated the national autonomy and integrity of Yugoslavia. Following the end of warlike hostilities, the Western military alliance established the Kosovo Force (KFOR) to maintain the peace with the Kosovo Republic and especially its northern border with the Serbian population centers (Hendrickson 2006, 94–105). The EU changed its own structure in defense in 1999, by adding a program entitled the European Security and Defense Policy (ESDP). The triple involvement of the UN, NATO, and the EU underlined regional and global concerns about the continuance of war in the Balkans during the first decade after the end of the Cold War.

UN management of Kosovo included a considerable presence of outside military forces, even though the NATO operation had only included an aerial component. Under the UN banner, NATO organized a 17,000 KFOR military contingent, while the EU added another 1,800 military trainers to the Kosovo Republic under the heading ALTHEA-EUFOR. Just as in Bosnia several years earlier, the newest NATO members including the Czech Republic, Hungary, and Poland all contributed to the effort to preserve the peace in Kosovo. Eventually, the additional new East European NATO members admitted in 2004 all made contributions to that defense force as well. Those alliance members included Estonia, Latvia, Lithuania, Slovakia, Slovenia, Romania, and Bulgaria (Štěpanovský 2008,

18–22). Such a strong and multi-pronged military involvement provided clear evidence of Western hopes to prevent Balkan nationalism from causing additional and extensive bloodshed.

In 2008, Kosovo declared its independence as a state, and general Western recognition occurred in a step-by-step fashion. Of course, neither Serbia nor Russia offered them diplomatic recognition, and some of their allies followed suit with non-recognition. Examination of the Kosovo Constitution reveals the extent to which the leaders of the new state endeavored to provide protection for both Serbs and Kosovars in ways that would preserve the peace within the new country. For example, in Article 5 there is a clear statement that the Albanian and Serbian languages maintained the same co-equal status. At the municipal level, Article 8 additionally guaranteed protection for the language rights of the Roma, Turkish, and Bosnian minorities.

Design of the Parliament bore the same effort to preserve the rights of all groups in the new state. There were 120 seats overall, and 20 were guaranteed for members of the minority groups. Serbs would select the members for 10 of those seats, Bosnians 3, and the Turks 2, with the others scattered among smaller groups. Importantly, this body with its careful nationalistic balance had the right to control the composition of the rest of the executive branch. They also had considerable control of the components of the executive branch as well. For instance, the parliamentary assembly chose the president as well as five deputy presidents. While three of those deputies would be Albanians, one would be a Serb, and one would be from the additional ethnic groups in the nation. That legislatively chosen president would then propose who the prime minister should be, and that person could pick the Cabinet. The Cabinet would have roughly a dozen persons in it, and there was a guarantee that one of them would be a Serb. Perhaps this tightly knit legislative-executive governmental structure was to be both a counterpoint to and brake against the outbreak of further unrest. Interestingly, the Supreme Court as well as Appeals Courts guaranteed that 15 percent of their positions would be for non-majority communities, but there was no constitutional assurance that Serbs would be represented on it (Assembly-Kosovo 2008).

Nationalism was very much in evidence in all of these political issues related to Kosovo. It drove the civil war in 1998–99, the careful attention to the preservation of stability by three global organizations, and the written features of constitutional power for the various groups.

## Civil War in Macedonia, 2001

Macedonia (now North Macedonia) is an East European state with a Slavic majority of 60 percent but also a sizeable 40 percent Albanian minority. Ethnonationalism was apparent after its emergence as an independent state, for twenty political parties immediately emerged, with "most of them committed to ethnopolitical goals." The Party of Democratic Prosperity was the main representative of the Albanian minority (Cohen 1993, 147–48). Very quickly Macedonia became "a tinderbox of the Balkans," in part because of the traditional Greek view that Macedonia was properly part of their state and did not deserve to be one on its own. In fact, the UN brought in peacekeeping troops that included several hundred from the United States as early as 1994, in part to prevent Macedonia from becoming another Bosnia that had experienced at that time a two-year tough civil war (Hupchick 1995, 159).

Near civil war ensued somewhat later in spring 2001, just before the 9/11 attacks in the United States, and part of the reason was serious talk about linking together the 25 percent Albanian minority in Macedonia with the country of Albania and the then Republic of Kosovo into a unified Greater Albania. Serbian resistance was powerful, but so was the negative attitude of the non-Albanian majority in Macedonia. The Ohrid Agreement settled matters and at least created stability in the short term within the state. Albanians received considerable rights in the redefined state to include the use of their language in schools and other public settings.

## Moldova and Its Transdniestrian Russian Minority

Like the three Baltic states, Moldova had been a republic in the Soviet Union, and it also contained a significant Russian minority in its eastern Transdniestrian region. Life in that region was totally immersed in Russian culture, and this did not fit well with the Romanian cultural flavor that characterized Moldova. Moldovan leaders clearly articulated their special hopes for an independent role in the region, and stable relations with Romania pulled them toward a western center of gravity rather than a Eurasian one. However, the presence of their Russian minority always provided a pull to the east and towards their former Russian orbit. Thus, there was a "high level of Russian influence and ambiguity on Moldova's long-term political alignment." For the West, the Transdniestrian enclave was a perennial part of "Europe's insecurity zone" (Lubecki and Peterson 2021, 159–60). It is no surprise that later Russian aggression in the region stirred up concerns in the West about the future of Transdniestria and its home in Moldova as well. Would Russia invade nearby Transdniestria as it had in Georgia's South Ossetia and Abkhazia in 2008? In effect, both territories in the northern part of Georgia had then become part of the Russian sphere of influence (Peterson 2013, 8). Even more pressing was the awakening of concerns about that ethnic Russian slice of Moldova during the Russian war in Ukraine in 2022. If Russia gained control of the land bridge from the Donbas, through Crimea, and into the area that included Odesa, there was a possibility of pushing further west into the Transdniestrian territory of Moldova. Overall, this situation also entailed conflict among various nationalisms to include those of Moldova, Russia, and perhaps even Romania.

## *Bulgaria and Its Turkish Minority*

Bulgaria had a substantial Turkish minority that constituted 10 percent of its population and that required continuous political and administrative attention. The Turkish minority was an inheritance from the days when Bulgaria was part of the Ottoman Empire (Peterson 2013, 134). In the 1990s, at one point the government stirred up local Turkish nationalism by changing place names within local Turkish communities into Bulgarian (Bell 1993, 96–98). After the Arab Spring of 2011, the Turkish minority sought to model its aspirations and goals after those Arabic groups who had rebelled against authoritarianism in North Africa. Some moved back across the sea to Turkey, but others clamored for attention to democratic rights in Bulgaria. For the most part, the Bulgarian leadership was responsive, and the situation remained calm. Sub-nationalist aspirations did not disappear but meshed in some ways with the Slavic system into which history had made them an integral part.

## Legacy Theory, Divergence Theory, Public Management Theory

Legacy Theory offers the best approach for understanding these ethnic conflicts within the post-communist states, for those differences are deeply rooted in history. Two such legacies offer powerful tools for analysis of this representation of nationalism in Eastern Europe. One legacy is the mix of Slavic and Albanian/Muslim peoples in the former Yugoslavia. Substantial such minorities lived in the Republics of Bosnia-Herzegovina, Macedonia, and Serbia. In some ways they co-existed in peaceful ways for many decades, but the break-up of Yugoslavia in the early 1990s spun off a new legacy of rivalry, conflict, and war. A second legacy is the scattering of Russians throughout the countries that have replaced former Soviet republics. In addition, the two legacies are reminders that Divergence Theory was often the dominant force in these struggles among very different peoples who lived so close together. Why did such divergencies among the ethnic groups remain below the surface during communist times but lead to military conflict after the shield of Yugoslavia was gone? Nationalism is part of the explanation, for many of these groups sought new national homes that would replace former ones that were a legacy of their communist past. On a more hopeful note, Public Management Theory can offer possible long-term answers to the important question of how to preserve a balance between state stability and fairness to all groups living within the borders of the countries. Structuring of political institutions, creativity in the design of executive positions, and inclusion of minority languages in official discourse can reduce the stress of dealing with so many competing ethnic nationalities in the name of broader nation-state viability.

## Migratory Pressures from the External Environment

Globalization also affected the ethnic composition of East European states through the occasional but often heavy flows of a diversity of migrant peoples into the region. A Roma presence was characteristic of many of the states, and governments continuously struggled with the need to assist the families in the presence of considerable nationalist resistance to their location in various communities. These groups, plus many others, migrated from state to state in the early Cold War period. This issue peaked during the COVID-19 crisis, as some regional governments resisted the provision of adequate supplies of needed medical equipment to the Roma communities. In 2015–16, thousands of refugees from the wars in Syria, Afghanistan, and Iraq came into Eastern Europe for protection and assistance or as a transition point to more prosperous states further north and west in Europe. More than six million refugees made it into more western countries after the invasion by Russia of Ukraine on February 24, 2022. The pressure was very great on border states such as Poland and Slovakia to find housing and a support system for those troubled peoples. In a sense, Chaos Theory was pertinent as a symbol of both the suddenness of the crises and the unpreparedness for strategies to deal with the new persons in their midst in each of these three settings. Public Management Theory offered some guidance on how to structure the overall approach to these unexpected problems from the outside environment, while Public Policy Theory provided some specifics about how to coordinate responsive strategies among the NATO/EU partners within the various parts of Eastern Europe.

### Immediate Post–Cold War Period

Immediate post–Cold War Roma migration, as a globalization force, had affected many countries in Europe, both East and West. The groups pretty much stuck to themselves and preserved cultures that were quite different from the predominant ones in their new states. However, their economic situation was often one that was weak and

## Ethnic Challenges Within and Without

in need of outside support from state bureaucracies. Thus, their presence often provoked resentment and nationalist outbursts from the traditional populations of the various states. It was expected that many of them would move to more prosperous settings in the western part of Europe after the end of the Cold War, but often that did not happen. As a result, it was often a challenge for the newly fashioned states of the region to provide basic needs such as medical and food supplies to them. Special treatment of them, of course, provoked sharp reactions from the majority groups in the state that also were struggling to meet basic economic needs.

After 1991, there was also considerable migration of assorted groups into individual East European states as well as into countries outside the region. However, the Dayton Agreement of 1995 prevented any refugees from the old Yugoslavia from migrating into the outlying East European states. In the Baltic states, there had been a huge influx of Russians from the Soviet Union, and that migratory force had been ongoing since 1945. Estonia had received 1.4 million Soviet citizens in that time frame, and they constituted 30.3 percent of the population by 1998. It is also the case that 100,000 had returned to Russia by 1998 (European Parliament Working Paper 1998, 25–27). Several million Russians entered Latvia during the post–WWII era, but many of them also went back home after 1991. Their illegal immigrants included persons from Russia, Belarus, and Ukraine (European Parliament Working Paper 1998, 36–40). Lithuania also experienced a lively movement of peoples, but it became a waiting room for migrants who were really headed in other directions such as the EU (European Parliament Working Paper 1998, 41–45).

East Central European states also endeavored to cope with other aspects of the migration issue, for they had not experienced the Russian influx that the states to the north had when they were republics in the Soviet Union. The Czech Republic became a transit state with many persons moving in from Bulgaria and Romania. However, for many of those people the ultimate goal was a new life in West Europe. In the period 1992–97, however, a full 206,577 people stayed in the Czech Republic and were content with the benefits provided to them (European Parliament Working Paper 1998, 16–24).

106　　　**Ethnic Challenges Within and Without**

The pattern for Hungary was similar and the term most appropriate was that they had become a "springboard" state. Interestingly, the main migrant group consisted of persons who were from Romania but ethnically Hungarian (54,000). The Chinese emigrant wave was also large at 10,000 (European Parliament Working Paper 1998, 28–35). For Poland, both the Balkan Trail and the Lithuanian Trail were busy after the end of the Cold War. Through the former came many Romanians, and through the latter individuals from Afghanistan, Iraq, Iran, India, Pakistan, and Sri Lanka. However, the target for both sets of migrants was ultimately Germany, and so Poland served also as a transit or springboard state (European Parliament Working Paper 1998, 46–51). Economic immigrants were the biggest source of the 464,000 illegals who entered Slovakia in the 1993–98 period. They traveled into the state from Yugoslavia, Afghanistan, Iraq, China, Vietnam, Sri Lanka, and India. After 1994, many of them wanted to remain in Slovakia, and so it did not serve exclusively as a transit state (European Parliament Working Paper 1998, 57–62).

Slovenia was a target as well as supplier of migrants from nearby states. Most appeared after trips from the former Yugoslavia and Romania, and their higher status as a receiving state gradually changed them from transit to target (European Parliament Working Paper 1998, 63). This was not a surprise in light of their high level of economic and educational standards. Bulgaria had a relatively low number of clandestine residents (5,000–10,000), and they permitted most to work without permits. Most of them came from the Middle East and Indian subcontinent (European Parliament Working Paper 1998, 10–15). Romania had provided many migrants to the states to the north, but it also had received many illegals from the Middle East, and most of them were heading towards Germany (European Parliament Working Paper 1998, 52–56).

## *Migration from the Middle East into Eastern Europe, 2015–16*

Movement of peoples from nearby countries in turmoil towards and into Eastern Europe in 2015–16 was a globalization force that led to

# Ethnic Challenges Within and Without

outcries and turmoil in the target countries. It was clear how the globalization process accounted for this huge influx of troubled and afflicted peoples. Some came from Afghanistan, a country that had been in turmoil and war for a decade and a half after the al Qaeda attack on the United States in September 2001. Clearly, the tensions centered on the civil conflict among Western-backed Afghans, the remnant of al Qaeda, and the rising ISIS threat. Other refugees were fleeing the continuing stress from the war in Iraq, even though the United States had withdrawn its active military forces in 2011. Syria's civil war continued, with the Assad regime contending with the majority Sunni opponents of his Alawite regime, Kurds, and ISIS/ISIL terrorists. Strong outside powers such as the United States and Russia saw fit to enter the conflict as well, ostensibly to provide stability but often contributing to the uncertainty of policy outcomes within the fabric of the Syrian state.

Most of these refugees came across the Mediterranean Sea and moved first into the southernmost states of Eastern Europe. Some were interested in locating temporary homes there, but many had more prosperous states such as Germany and Sweden in mind. Hungary was especially tough as its leaders constructed a barbed wire fence across its entire southern border to keep the refugees out of their territory. At the same time, they did permit train transit of many of these victims of Middle East wars into more western cities such as Munich, Germany. The Germans, under Chancellor Angela Merkel, received them with compassion and even provided toys for their children. EU efforts to assign a quota of refugees to European countries, based on population, received mixed messages from the East European members. However, many of the states took on those responsibilities in tune with their capabilities. In some of the states, populist nationalists waved the banner of celebrating the glory of their state at the expense of the refugees and their families. However, political discussions with most of the states generated reasonable compromises that reflected a sense or conclusion that they would care for the families in need.

The refugee crisis clearly brought the tension between globalization and nationalism to a head, for the migrants were an international force that put great pressure on borders while the reactions of recipient states often reflected powerful nationalist emotions (Peterson and Kuck 2017, 3–4). The explosion of ISIS in 2014 pointed toward the creation of a Caliphate that would include parts of Syria and Iraq. However, the Arab Spring in 2011 had set up turmoil across the region that percolated to a very high level with the later and sudden appearance of ISIS. Therefore, many people from those countries were on the move toward other nations in which they could have security, steady jobs, and basic resources (Anderson and O'Dowd 1999, 594). The numbers of refugees were very high, as they included 4.8 million from Syria, 4.7 million from Iraq, and 1.7 million from Afghanistan (Peterson and Kuck, 2017).

The Hungarian reaction was the strongest in Eastern Europe, as its Prime Minister Viktor Orbán had a 100-mile razor wall built on its border with the justification that incoming Muslims were a threat to the Christian culture that was predominant in Hungary (Dominique, March 24, 2022). Many migrants passed through the Keleti train station in Budapest but were denied the use of Hungarian trains to move to the west. Over 1,000 of them walked the 300 miles to the Austrian border before Orbán decided that they should be able to use buses (Peterson and Kuck 2017, 10). With the Hungarian border closed to the refugees, it became incumbent on nearby states to make decisions about their borders. After receiving 8,000 people across their border in one day, Croatia made a decision to redirect them to either Slovenia or Hungary. Hungary, of course, complained and Slovenia built its own fence, as did Macedonia. Effectively, these states had invented restrictions that closed the Balkan Trail at the time of the 2016 huge refugee flow that brought with it a new worry about potential terrorist acts by some of the newcomers. Another side effect of the migration was the number of boat accidents and deaths in the trip across the Aegean Sea. The EU and Turkey wrote a new agreement that restricted the number of migrants who took that trip (Peterson and Kuck 2017, 10–11).

EU quotas became another huge issue for the states of Eastern Europe, as that alliance allocated a number to each state for the expected quantity of refugees for which they had responsibility. Hungary held a referendum on the question of its allocation, and the vote was 98 percent "no" on admission of refugees. However, the

## Ethnic Challenges Within and Without

voter turnout was only 43.9 percent, and that was not high enough to reject the quota for them. The Visegrad Four (Czech Republic, Slovakia, Poland, and Hungary) went so far as to file a lawsuit at the EU Court of Justice in opposition to the imposed quotas. Eventually, the EU itself took a vote on the quota plan, and it passed 23-4-1, which led to the acceptance of them by the Czech Republic, Poland, and Romania. It must also be admitted that resistance to the quotas did not pivot only around the issue of the refugees in 2015–16, for the disastrous Balkan Wars of the 1990s created doubt and hesitation on the issue for both leaders and publics. This was especially the case for Serbia, Macedonia, Kosovo, and Bosnia; states that had borne the brunt of the earlier suffering and losses (Peterson and Kuck 2017, 13–14).

Analysts attempted to frame all of these events and challenges to Europe within their traditional value system. For instance, the President of the European Commission Jean-Claude Juncker articulated that the free movement of migrants was in tune with European values. The organization also tried to be practical by focusing the attention of the target nations on concrete issues such as trade, economic growth, and border security (Peterson and Kuck 2017, 14–15). East European resistance to the refugees led some to conclude that the experience of those states under communism had made them reluctant to embrace traditional European values (Gille 2017, 286). There had been an expectation by traditional members of the EU that their new post-communist members would quickly undergo convergence with their own value system, but the migrant crisis forced the leadership of the EU to question that assumption (Krastev 2017, 292). For example, the Slovak leader Robert Fico spoke of only accepting Christians since there were no mosques in Slovakia. Jaroslav Kaczński in Poland warned that the new residents in their state brought with them considerable health risks. Overall, the experience of the post-communist states in their first few decades after 1989 had generated a general "mistrust of institutions." Members and leaders of these states remembered how difficult it had been in recent decades to integrate the Roma, and now an even greater challenge had occurred. Mistrust of the "cosmopolitan mindset" was part of the local resentment, and it was no surprise

**110**                    **Ethnic Challenges Within and Without**

that a "renationalization of sentiment" was a direct result (Krastev 2017, 293–96).

## Ukrainian Refugee Migration during Russian War on Ukraine, 2022

In early 2022, the Russian unexpected and unjustified invasion of its neighbor Ukraine stimulated the departure of millions of refugees into nearby East European states. Poland, Moldova, Slovakia, and Romania were the border states with Ukraine and thus received the highest number of Ukrainians seeking sanctuary, perhaps temporarily, in a place other than their homeland. In addition to this external migration from Ukraine, there were large numbers of Ukrainians who became internal refugees within their own country and moved to different locations there. Poland received, by far, the highest number of refugees, as had Germany during the 2015–16 movement of peoples. Many of the refugees hoped eventually to return to Ukraine, but there was no clear target date when that might occur. Reception of the migrant Ukrainians was warm, as there were many persons from that state who had moved west in earlier years. West European states took them in, as did the United States and Canada. However, many of the Ukrainians who moved out of their state wanted to remain close by or with family members who were already in Poland and the other recipient countries. Given the difficult economic situation during the COVID-19 crisis, it was no small matter for the host nations to settle in the newcomers and provide their needs in terms of jobs, food supplies, child-rearing support, education, and health benefits.

In 2022, the migration pattern following the Russian invasion of Ukraine, and the East European response to it, was much warmer to these new residents than was their reaction to the outsiders who crossed their borders in 2015–16.

From a glance at Table 4.1, it is clear that there has been considerable willingness of the East European states to accept Ukrainian refugees without any quotas imposed by global organizations such as the EU or even NATO. According to the UN, twelve million Ukrainians had fled their homes since the commencement of

## Ethnic Challenges Within and Without

**Table 4.1** Number of refugees admitted by states in the region of Ukraine, 2022.

| | |
|---|---|
| Russia | 1,305,018 |
| Poland | 1,180,018 |
| Moldova | 85,797 |
| Romania | 82,733 |
| Slovakia | 78,972 |
| Hungary | 25,042 |
| Belarus | 9,006 |
| Germany | 780,000 |
| Czech Republic | 380,000 |
| Italy | 137,000 |

Source: BBC News, June 30, 2022.

the war in late February, and five million of those persons were in nearby countries, while the majority were in new locations within Ukraine. More than half of those who had fled Ukraine had actually returned to their home country, after it became clear that Russian military attacks were mainly confined to the east of the country. The EU had been very receptive to the newcomers and did all possible to make their lives workable and even comfortable. The migrants could remain in EU states for up to three years and could work there as well. They also would receive benefits such as food, medical care, social welfare payments, housing, and education (BBC News, June 30, 2022; Dominique, March 24, 2022). In contrast to the 2015 icy reception to the refugees from three Middle Eastern states as well as to the 2021 Middle Easterners who came through Belarus to Poland, charities in both Poland and Hungary reached out with warmth to the Ukrainians in 2022 (Dominique, March 24, 2022). However, memories from the past still stick in the recipient states for the Ukrainian Insurgent Army had massacred many Poles in border regions during WWII. Further, Hungarian culture and language were very different from their Ukrainian counterparts, and older Hungarians still remembered the invasion by Soviet troops as well as Ukrainians in 1956 in an effort to stamp out their reform movement (Dominique, March 24, 2022). In sum, the reaction in

East European states to the suddenness and horror of the Russian attack on Ukraine of February 24, 2022, as well as its aftermath, overrode any such hesitation by the recipient states.

## Theoretical Conclusion

Given the suddenness of the war and Ukrainian migration, Chaos Theory provides immediate insights for the refugee crisis that spun off from the 2022 Russian-Ukrainian War. All the occurrences connected with that war were so unexpected that all parties to the conflict were set back on their heels with responses uncertain and spinning in the heads of the leaders. Public Management Theory applied to all three sets of refugee challenges, for it provided some guidance about how executive administrators in the recipient states could work the new residents into existing local, regional, and national social assistance organizations. Further, Public Policy Theory was helpful, for steps taken by the host countries in 2015–16 to relocate the newcomers could serve as a model for the 2022 outflow of peoples from Ukraine. Policy steps could be repeated until the worst of the crisis settled down.

# Chapter 5

# DOMESTIC AND GLOBAL
# SECURITY CHALLENGES

*JAMES W. PETERSON*

## Terrorist Threats inside the State

Threats to domestic security periodically occurred from sources that were certainly non-

nationalist in origin but that soon became part of the fabric of national life. The September 11, 2001, attacks by al Qaeda on American soil created a concern within the individual states of Eastern Europe that similar events could take place on their territories, and indeed some did. Similarly, the rise of ISIS after 2014 led to imitating events that the terror groups either caused or inspired, and these became urgent national issues and concerns. There were, of course, repeated terrorist attacks within the Balkan states during their civil wars, and these were usually linked to the ethnic complexity of each state and the intense challenge of Serbian incursions into their midst. The rise of authoritarian governments within a select handful of East European states also generated, when permitted, public protests that at times entailed violent actions. Clearly, regime-sponsored threats against those protestors bore the hallmark of overtly, ultra-nationalist expressions of the ultimate need to keep the nation-state in line and stable. Realist Theory represents a hard-headed approach to the decision-making process, and this very much is applicable to the governmental thinking about responding to these challenges. For the leaders, idealism has no place in these struggles. The creation of a system that can control and even prevent some of these threats and challenges is also pertinent, and Systems Theory offers a dependable framework that carefully balances inputs and outputs in ways that can raise the hope of security and stability in the future. The development of new Public Policies is probably a long-term prospect but one

**114**      **Domestic and Global Security Challenges**

that needs attention in the middle and long-term periods if not the short-term ones.

## *Overview of Key Nation-State Themes and Terrorism*

The al Qaeda threat after 2001 bore many implications for the states of Eastern Europe, as they worried that such a group might hit them as well. After all, they were allies of the United States, three had joined the North Atlantic Treaty Organization (NATO) in 1999, and several others were in line to do so in 2004. The only Muslim-majority state was Albania, while Bosnia-Herzegovina had a Muslim plurality but one that was under huge pressure from nearby Serbs. All the rest were vulnerable to potential Muslim terrorist group pressures within their own states. After the American invasion of Afghanistan in late 2001, the concern was the dislodgement of the Taliban government that had provided sanctuary to al Qaeda. Most states of Eastern Europe supported that US-led allied effort, and many provided troops and humanitarian assistance to the NATO mission in the country. Those East European states did experience casualties, but the hope was deterrence of al Qaeda attacks within their own states.

In the period after 2014, ISIS/ISIL became the principal concern about committing crimes on behalf of the Muslim terrorists, and this threat had a powerful impact on all states of Europe. France experienced a devastating attack, and the leaders of surrounding countries shared concerns about similar explosions on their own soil. Did they possess the security systems and tools to prevent or control such attacks? The states of Eastern Europe were all part of the Western culture against which the terrorists directed their hatred and tactics. In addition, the military involvement of the states of the region in the American-led efforts in both Iraq and Afghanistan enhanced their vulnerability to that category of terrorists. It is also the case that citizens within any of the East European states could become dissatisfied with their own governments, become active on key terrorist internet sites, and work with outside ISIS members to create violent events in their own homeland. Control of such homegrown individual terrorists would have sharply challenged

## Domestic and Global Security Challenges

especially the leadership of smaller states such as Estonia, Slovenia, or Macedonia.

Four countries in the Balkans experienced difficult civil wars in the seven years between 1992 and 1999. Such violent outbreaks were surprising and disturbing after the relatively quiet end to the Cold War at the beginning of that decade. In order, the civil wars took place in Slovenia, Croatia, Bosnia-Herzegovina, and Kosovo which was then a Republic in the shrunken state of Yugoslavia. Within each of those geographic units, violent incidents occurred that took civilian lives and certainly verged on the category of terrorist acts. Of course, the worst suffering took place in Bosnia-Herzegovina, and evidence of massacres placed very heavy responsibility on the Serbs. Since the victims in such tragedies were primarily Muslims, there was always the possibility of attacks by the growing groups like al Qaeda into the territories of such victimized states. While Serbs received much of the blame for the violent episodes in all four geographic units, there is also evidence of violence by the groups they targeted against them. There was also a need for outside assistance from NATO and the European Union (EU) in both military and rebuilding efforts with an eye on the preservation of renewed state security in the Balkans.

At times, protests on purely domestic issues took place in the states of the region. Such outbursts were likely in countries that contained sizeable minority groups, economic challenges, and at times authoritarian leadership. Most of these new democracies had changeable political party systems and frequent election-based governmental changes. Protests and demonstrations were a fact of life and sometimes entailed security questions and issues. For example, in 2008–9, demonstrators in the Czech Republic protested their government's agreement with the Bush Administration in Washington for a Missile Defense System. Poland and the Czech Republic were to be the sites for the location of the infrastructure for a protective system against potential nuclear threats from Iran or another unpredictable state. In the end, the Obama Administration canceled the plan and developed another NATO-based proposal to include Romania and Poland. Such challenges did not evoke the fear of terrorism but did undercut the efforts of state leaders to evolve an overall sense of security in the state.

Sometimes, the new democracies of Eastern Europe moved in authoritarian directions, in part due to the preservation of a subject political culture during the communist period. It is also the case that the countries of Southeast Europe took more time to move away from the authoritarian complexion of their communist-era past than did the more economically developed states in the Baltics and East Central Europe. In this framework, the political leadership often took firm steps against any public protests that did occur. Further, authoritarianism often characterized leadership responses to the pandemic of the 2020–22 period. It was the case that the Roma at times did not receive medical supplies and attention to the extent that the rest of the population did. There were also situations in which areas that had voted against the incumbent government suffered as they received less medical attention than did areas that had been willing to vote for the sitting authorities. Such actions created uncertainty and anxiety within the population of the state and were a challenge or even threat to security.

## *Problem of Terrorism*

One indicator that demonstrates the preoccupation of the East European states with terrorism was their involvement in the war in Afghanistan after 2001. As many East European states became members of NATO early in the twenty-first century, there was an obligation under Article 5 to do so. Many of their troops did serve in more peaceful regions of the country such as its western portion, but others played key roles in defending the key airports in Afghanistan. Dispatch of medical professionals and teachers was also an important function of these new alliance partners. Given both the uncertain loyalty of some of their Afghan military partners on these projects and the constant incidents of explosive attacks, there was no guarantee that casualties would not result from their military involvement and commitments. As Table 5.1 reveals, the countries of Eastern Europe suffered 112 deaths in the combat zones of Afghanistan.

# Domestic and Global Security Challenges

**Table 5.1** East European casualties in Afghanistan.

| Country | Number of casualties |
|---|---|
| Poland | 44 |
| Romania | 26 |
| Czech Republic | 14 |
| Estonia | 9 |
| Hungary | 7 |
| Latvia | 4 |
| Slovakia | 3 |
| Albania | 1 |
| Bulgaria | 1 |
| Croatia | 1 |
| Lithuania | 1 |
| Montenegro | 1 |
| *Total* | *112* |

Source: *Wikipedia* 2022a.

Part of the explanation for such involvement and such sacrifices was the obligations of NATO for the full partners and for the candidate members. However, all the leaders of the various states also hoped that suppression and defeat of terrorists in Afghanistan would prevent incursions and outbreaks of the Taliban and al Qaeda in their own states. Protection of their own people was thus an important national goal through this challenging commitment of their own soldiers.

The Balkan Wars from 1993 to 1999 brought actual terrorist actions into their own borders and territories, although all the perpetrators and key actors were from those states. Bosnia-Herzegovina was the centerpiece of most of these tragedies, and the horrors resulted from the acts of aggression by Serbs from the shrunken Yugoslavia as well as by the Bosnian Serbs, mainly against Muslim Albanians who constituted a plurality of the population in that state. There were very serious charges that the Serbs were guilty of "ethnic cleansing," and the most egregious example of that violation of post–WWII values and institutions was the Srebrenica Massacre of 1995. The 26,000-person United Nations Protection Force (UNPROFOR) worked under the restriction that they could not take on offensive combat operations in the areas they supervised. Thus, the Dutch UN contingent that held the main responsibility for guarding the area was helpless when the Bosnian Serbs carted many Albanians off to the countryside (Roskin 2002, 176). As a result, 8,000 Muslims were killed. The Bosnian Serbian forces claimed that they were all Albanian soldiers against whom they were fighting, but later evidence unearthed by a reporter for the *Christian Science Monitor* revealed that there were crutches and children's toys in the field where all had been buried. Clearly, this was an act of terrorism, and an international outcry occurred whenever the names of the perpetrators Milošević, Mladić, or Karadžić came up.

There was a concerted regional effort to punish those responsible for the atrocities. The Stabilisation Force (SFOR) replaced the Implementation Force (IFOR) in managing the country in 1996, and one of their principal goals was the prosecution of war criminals, and they were successful in that endeavor, as the key perpetrators did end up at the War Crimes Tribunal in The Hague. In 2004, the European Union Force (EUFOR) took over that responsibility, and the EU essentially replaced NATO in watching for potential terrorist intentions or even actions (Peterson 2011, 64). Bosnia-Herzegovina thus experienced in its early nationalist phase a terrible challenge to its efforts to create a state but also substantial outside assistance in coping with terrorism that was so antithetical to the burgeoning forces of domestic nationalism. Clearly, domestic security was a profound issue that entailed competing nationalisms within the new state and a tough challenge to establish a sense of national loyalties and bonds.

Kosovo in 1998–99 was both similar to and very different from Bosnia in its struggles. On the one hand, Serbs and Albanians were the rival groups and sets of combatants. Charges of ethnic cleansing emerged in that battle zone as they had in Bosnia. Serbs had moved south in an effort to control more firmly the large Muslim community that lived in the region that contained the birthplace of the founding of the Serbian Orthodox Church as well as its historic battle ground of Kosovo Pole. However, the domestic complexion of the struggle was quite different than it was in Bosnia. In Bosnia, Serbs

## Domestic and Global Security Challenges

from the country of Yugoslavia had moved into the new nation of Bosnia-Herzegovina in an effort to support the aggressive efforts of Bosnian Serbs against the Albanians. However, Kosovo was a republic in the shrunken but Serb-dominated state of Yugoslavia. Efforts by the West to repel the Serbs would have constituted interference within a state rather than against an outside aggressor. In spite of that difference President Clinton worked with NATO to order air strikes against Serbian positions, and that brought an end to the actual war itself. Part of the urgency that led to NATO involvement at all was the understanding that they had probably waited too long to involve themselves in the Bosnian War. As a result, casualties had mounted to very unacceptable levels, and there was unanimity among the Western allies that the same result should not happen in Kosovo (Jentleson 2007, 288–89).

Following the end of the conflict in 1999, three international organizations shared in the administration of Kosovo to prevent repeated outbreaks of violence. The UN was in charge of overall management, while NATO controlled the 17,000 military Kosovo Force (KFOR), to which a full thirty-four nations contributed. The EU provided 1,800 military personnel who took on functions such as training the Kosovo police (Štěpanovský 2008, 18–22). Following the 9/11 attacks on the United States, there was a perception among some in Eastern Europe that their presence in Kosovo was even more needed, for prevention of unpredictable terrorism was vital in each setting (Peterson 2011, 72). Ironically, NATO scaled back its presence in Kosovo to 10,000 personnel in order to transfer more of its capabilities to the war against terrorism in Afghanistan. Obviously, both the Balkan Wars and the struggle in Afghanistan pointed to the need for a stronger framework of security in coping with the growing specter of terrorism (Kelly 2007, Abstract).

In addition, all seventeen states of Eastern Europe occasionally experienced their own threats of Middle East–based terrorism. In the time frame from 1970 to 2016, the most occurred in Macedonia and Kosovo. There were also fourteen in Bosnia-Herzegovina, ten in Albania, and ten in Croatia. All the other states experienced numbers that were much lower in the single digits (*Washington Post*

2022). No doubt, that threat was more evident in the Balkans than in the northern sectors of the region.

In at least six of the states, there was a concern about potential acts of terrorist violence that were very focused. For example, some Albanians became foreign terrorist fighters and left their state to join rebellions in Iraq and Syria. Once they returned home to Albania, there was a concern that they might radicalize the youth of the country. In 2018, the Albanian state police prevented an Iranian attack on its Albanian-located opposition group Mujahedeen-e-Khalq (MEK). The government and managers of Bosnia-Herzegovina had concerns about the fact that some of their citizens had joined the wars in Iraq, Syria, and Ukraine. What attitudes would accompany them upon their return to their home state?

Bulgarian leaders had a number of similar threats to consider, even though they had tried to prevent their outbursts through the construction of a razor wire fence along most of their border with Turkey. In June 2019, they arrested a student who had made plans to carry out a terrorist attack in Plovdiv. At that time, court cases were still ongoing on a 2012 attack by Hizballah on Burgas Airport. In the fall of 2019, Bulgarian prosecutors indicted five Syrians and one Bulgarian for terrorist financing. They had transferred $10 million in order to send 100 vehicles to support terrorists in Syria who operated near the border with Turkey. In December of that year, officials in the city of Pazrdzhik sentenced the Islamic preacher Ahmed Mussa and thirteen of his followers in the Roma Muslim community. Mussa received a four-year sentence for working with ISIS and stoking religious hatred within the community.

Even Kosovo, with such a strong and stabilizing international presence, experienced terrorist incidents. In 2019, officials arrested six persons who were planning terrorist attacks in other states as well as within Kosovo against KFOR troops, night clubs, and Serb Orthodox churches. The lead defendant in that case received a ten-year prison sentence. In addition, they indicted another citizen who used social media to post support for terrorist attacks in Sri Lanka. Many citizens (156) from North Macedonia had gone to Syria and Iraq to operate as foreign terrorist fighters. More than half of them

## Domestic and Global Security Challenges

had returned home, and there was anxiety about any operation they might plan there (US Department of State 2019).

There were several terrorist acts and plots that affected more than one of the current states of Eastern Europe. In February 2001, the former state of Yugoslavia was the victim of the Podjevu bus bombing that resulted in twelve deaths and forty injured persons. Kosovo Albanian militants were suspected of carrying out that attack (*Wikipedia*2022c). In November 2016, Albania hosted a football game with the Israeli national team. There were eighteen arrests of persons from Kosovo, Albania, and Macedonia for their plans to attack the Israeli team (*Wikipedia* 2022b).

### *Rise of Authoritarian Leaders*

Another domestic factor that carried national security implications at times was the rise of certain authoritarian leaders within the states of Eastern Europe. There are several ways of characterizing these leaders and systems. One is "illiberal democracies" that have moved away from EU democratic values, and Poland and Hungary currently fit into that category. Such systems contrast with fully authoritarian political systems like Russia (Minakov 2020). Another potential label for those two states is that of "deepening autocratisation," the descriptive label that Freedom House (2021) has applied. Of course, many observers have simply stated that certain Eastern European states are either moving away from or towards "authoritarianism." Whatever the label, it is clear that these changes from the democratic orders that emerged after the end of communism can be destabilizing in the affected states.

What is the evidence that Poland and Hungary have moved in such a direction in ways that have created less security and more anxiety within their populations? Under Orbán in Hungary, the executive branch has sought to keep out immigrants with razor fences, cracked down on human rights groups, attacked media outlets, and restricted civic organizations. There was a major protest that consisted of thousands of Hungarian citizens on the occasion of a visit by Chancellor Merkel of Germany in February 2015. Similarly, in Poland, the Law and Justice Party was victorious in the October

2015 elections. Although the Constitutional Court ruled that the party could not replace five judges with their own sympathizers, the new government did so anyway. As a result, there were 50,000 protestors in the streets in the last month of the year (Carpenter 2015).

The above-mentioned Freedom House has reported similar results for both Poland and Hungary, as they have reported that both states experienced declines in the strength of democracy over the last seventeen years. Still, their general category for Poland was "democracy," but Hungary had sunk into the second category of a "hybrid regime." In addition to the regime steps noted above, this report also itemized attacks on the LGBT community, on ethnic minorities, and on certain religious groups (Freedom House 2021). While the emergent authoritarianism in certain East European states may not threaten lives as much as terrorist plots and attacks, that governmental trend certainly indicates a departure from existing democratic structures and participatory expectations.

## Theoretical Conclusion

Realist Theory is helpful in analyzing the above state-based challenges, for it calls upon leaders and their populations to think broadly about the overall national interest and resulting state security. Idealism about individual or group-based rights takes second place to that priority in such complicated situations. Systems Theory is also helpful for it suggests that an organized state response to and incorporation of inputs and desires from the people and their groups is essential in order to create outputs and outcomes that can enhance security. Behind these broad considerations lies Public Policy Theory with its heavy emphasis on steady leadership attention to the continued development of and evaluation of both old and needed new policies.

## Russian Imperial Challenges after Crimea Takeover, 2014

Global security challenges to Eastern Europe centered on Russian imperial ambitions

# Domestic and Global Security Challenges

that were on display during the takeover of Crimea in 2014 as well as the unexpected and unjustified invasion of Ukraine in 2022. The initial conquest provided a direct threat to regional powers that shared Black Sea borders with Russia, and those states included the regional players Bulgaria and Romania. This was especially disturbing as Russia added much more military equipment to its naval base in Sevastopol, a Crimean port on the Black Sea. The 2022 war that Russia initiated with Ukraine also raised the stakes of fear for selected states of Eastern Europe. The three Baltic states of Estonia, Latvia, and Lithuania were very close to Russia and had feared for several years Russian exploitation of their minorities in the three states in some way. The initial fears had centered on cyberwarfare, but after 2014, the anxiety escalated to include actual efforts to annex them. The Russian militarized exclave of Kaliningrad was located between Poland and Lithuania, and thus Polish concerns about an incursion by Russia increased as well. Many other issues penetrated the cloud of uncertainty about the rationale for the Russian invasion of Ukraine, and they included the future of Russian oil exports into the region via the Nordstream pipeline. Russian threats of the use of either chemical or nuclear weapons increased East European anxieties as well, due to their geographic proximity to the Russian border. Legacy Theory is appropriate in analyzing this tragic situation, for East European states had vivid memories of the Soviet control over their geographic space during the Cold War. Alliance Politics Theory was highly significant as well, for the NATO alliance of thirty members galvanized on behalf of both assistance to Ukraine and the buttressing of their presence in the states of the East European community. What could the Balance of Power be in the future? Engagement of this theory was a genuine conundrum, for renewal of some form of the old Cold War struggle that took place between the Soviet Union and its Warsaw Pact with the West and its key alliance NATO would be an unhappy as well as unappealing outcome to the states of Eastern Europe.

## Overview of Key Regional Pressures from Russia

President Putin's Russia engaged in a two-part effort to take over as much of Ukraine as was possible, both in 2014 and in 2022.

**124** **Domestic and Global Security Challenges**

In Part One in 2014, the capture of Crimea was an unexpected outcome of political conflict within Ukraine over the direction of its future alliances. President Yanukovych leaned towards more association with Russia at a time when many citizens of Ukraine had been expecting a move in a western direction and potential membership in the EU. The Maidan Revolt in Kyiv brought many protestors against the regime into the streets, and the police killed at least 100 of them. Very soon the Ukrainian president escaped to Russia, but Putin took advantage of the turmoil to work in a subversive way with the Russian ethnic group and leaders who were dominant in the Crimean Republic in Ukraine. At the time Russia portrayed the Russian takeover of Crimea as a product of purely local forces, but it was evident that Moscow had sent in its soldiers too. As a result, Putin quickly annexed Crimea, introduced the ruble as its currency, and declared it to be a formal Russian republic.

In 2022, Part Two of the Russian endeavor to gain control of Ukraine surprised the world, despite the long build-up of Russian troops on the border as well as in the Black Sea. The rationale for Putin was near impossible for most of the rest of the Western world to comprehend. In June 2020 he had written a long essay on the weakness of a West that capitulated to Hitler during the Munich Pact of 1938. He dismissed many of his critics who averred that the Soviet Union's Molotov-Ribbentrop Agreement of the following year was equally culpable for the rise and domination of Hitler in the region at the beginning of WWII. In retrospect, he was convening a strong view about the need to stand up to dangerous states and their leaders in the present. In July of 2021, Putin had written another essay with a totally direct link to Ukraine and the Russian-Ukrainian relationship. In it, he devoted many pages to the founding of Russia in the current Ukrainian capital of Kyiv. Further, the Russian Orthodox Church was first set up in the Crimean Peninsula near Sevastopol. He intimated that an effort to reunite Russia with the ancient locations central to its founding and meaning would be defensible. He did not really perceive there to be sound reasons for the independence of Russia's spiritual home in Ukraine, from Russia proper.

## Domestic and Global Security Challenges 125

In a sense, what Putin seemed to be saying was that his effort to take over Ukraine was a fulfillment of Russia's millennial-long history as well as the principal lessons from WWII. How could the Russian president make such an argument after three decades of Ukrainian independence from the former Soviet Union? Harking back to WWII, he said that it was necessary to de-Nazify Ukraine from its current leadership and spirit. However, there was no evidence of Nazism in 2022 Ukraine, and its President Zelenskyy was Jewish. Putin also contended that NATO had marched too closely to the Russian border and constituted a huge threat that would soon include Ukraine. It is true that NATO carefully considered Ukrainian alliance membership, as well as that of Georgia, at its Bucharest Summit in 2008. It is also the case that the NATO Program written in summer 2021 did include as goals both the restoration of Crimea to Ukraine and inclusion of Ukraine in the military alliance that had always maintained an open-door policy. However, there was no serious discussion of moves to include Ukraine in NATO in 2022 or in recent years. Overall, the Russian president's justification for the invasion of Ukraine, with all the ensuing suffering, loss of lives, and destruction was weak and persuasive only to members of his inner circle.

If Putin's goal was the conquest and absorption of Ukraine into Russia, such efforts fell short in the early months of the war. Ukrainians fought very hard and knew their terrain much better than did their Russian counterparts. Russia did attack the capital city of Kyiv after lining up miles of military vehicles before coming in to make that conquest, and they even hit sites near Lviv with their bombs. However, Ukrainian resilience coupled with the weaknesses in the Russian military as well as in its command structure prevented much success in those ventures. Thus, Russia re-centered its plans on a takeover of the Luhansk and Donbas regions that they had occupied since 2014. They also fought to create a land bridge across the east and south that would be a connector to Crimea. Control of the Black Sea and access to it would be a result. One of the greatest tragedies of this war was the fate of the city of Mariupol and particularly its base at Azovstal. Military and civilian personnel who had sought refuge there could not get out, and many of them

## 126 Domestic and Global Security Challenges

perished under the attacks and isolation. Eventually, some buses were able to take people west to safe havens, but the Russian troops also took many to Russia and turned many Ukrainian soldiers into Russian prisoners of war. It was clear that this struggle would continue for a long time with uncertain outcomes for both sides.

All these wartime developments were destabilizing for the countries of Eastern Europe, for it was unclear what limits Putin would recognize in relation to them. Would the small Baltic states experience additional cyberwarfare as they had in the past or even efforts to exploit their Russian minorities for the benefit of Moscow and its titans? Given the proximity of Moldova's Transdniestrian Russians to the so-called Russian land bridge in the south of Ukraine, would intervention there occur? In light of the many decades of Polish-Russian hostility, would Putin utilize their exclave of Kaliningrad, located between Poland and Lithuania, to undermine the Poles who had been the most hospitable state to Ukrainian refugees? Economic struggles also played a role in Putin's security calculus. A number of Eastern European states had become dependent on the Nordstream pipeline, and he threatened to cut off access to it for them. In fact, he did so towards Finland after that state and Sweden made clear their hopes to join NATO in response to the new meaning of the Russian threat. The Biden-led coalition had called for extreme sanctions of all NATO partners on Russia, and even the Germans who had been most linked to Nordstream bowed out of their imports from it. Hungary was the only holdout and continued to be in favor of receiving Russian oil and natural gas. In recent years, Putin had worked to restore Russia's relationship with China as a way of building an Asian coalition against the West. In reaction to the invasion of Ukraine, Western states put much pressure on China to be neutral in the war, and they had some success with those efforts. Eastern European states possessed some leverage with China on this target, for many of them had expanded both economic and cultural links in recent years under Chinese prodding.

### Concrete Post–Cold War Regional Roles for Russia

Western powers after 1991 perceived Russia to be a strong but lessened factor in regional and global relations than had been true

# Domestic and Global Security Challenges    127

during the Cold War. The Yeltsin Presidency of the 1990s reinforced that new image of Russia, for he struggled to maintain power within a new political system that contained a multiplicity of political parties with widely varying views. American President George H. W. Bush was relatively free to guide Western nations through the Persian Gulf war of 1990–91. NATO was relatively free to develop its Partnership for Peace program for newly freed Eastern European states, and American guidance was apparent in the choice of Vice President Albert Gore to manage the process. In a sense, this attitude persisted through the immediate aftermath of the 9/11 attacks. The new President Putin in Russia was sympathetic to America, offered help, and did not protest when Uzbekistan and Kyrgyzstan permitted use of their bases by American troops soon engaged in the war in Afghanistan.

## *Early Twenty-First-Century Emergence of Putin Leadership*

However, this cooperative Russian attitude disappeared during the first decade of the twenty-first century and became hostile as well as irrational. Timothy Frye explains this transformation by concluding that Russia possesses "an unusual autocracy in its foreign policy." Cold War Russian perceptions still guide foreign policy elites who are concerned with the preservation of the "great-power status" of the state. Kremlin elites are somewhat like Americans who see their country as "an exceptional country with a mission to spread its values" (Frye 2021, 152–60). There is also a sense that Putin views Russia historically as a Eurasian state rather than as part of East or West, and the formation of the Russian-inspired Eurasian Economic Union was a symbol of that spirit. It was far smaller than the EU but did include the important states of Russia, Belarus, Armenia, Kazakhstan, and Kyrgyzstan. From that vantage point, state borders are somewhat insignificant, for traditionally all kinds of ethnic and cultural groups have moved through the region and settled down for extended periods of time. It is only from such a self-perception that Putin could emerge with the conclusion, in 2022, that Ukraine is not really a country but simply another cultural group that is coupled with Russia in many inexplicable and nearly mysterious ways. Such beliefs led Putin to celebrate the 2014 conquest of Crimea with a speech to the Duma in which he explained these events as part of the glory of Russian history. He reminded his listeners that the conversion to Orthodoxy was a decision made by Prince Vladimir at a church in Crimea (Peterson 2017, 149–50). Crimea had now become another Russian Republic.

In 2004, Ukraine took a sharp turn towards the West with the advent to power of Viktor Yushchenko on the stream of the Orange Revolution. During his presidency the leadership expressed an interest in working with or even joining NATO and the EU. Some in the leadership made an effort to downplay the importance of Russian culture and language in modern-day Ukraine, in spite of the heavy Russian population in the east of the state as well as in Crimea. The presence of the Russian fleet in the Crimean port of Sevastopol was also a point of contention, and Ukrainian nationalists called for a timetable for the withdrawal of the fleet (Peterson 2013, 160–61). After all, how many nations hosted foreign military personnel and equipment at a significant base on their own territory? The Russian response to the implementation of the Orange Revolution was mainly negative. Thus, they supported the campaign and election to the Ukrainian presidency of Viktor Yanukovych in 2010, and this led to the unraveling of much of the work of the Yushchenko government. The new president nodded to the East rather than the West and made deals with Russia that were aimed at the preservation of natural gas deliveries as well as of the Russian naval presence at Sevastopol.

During the year 2008 there were two key events that reinforced the Russian self-image of regional and global importance. The Bush Administration had agreed with both Poland and the Czech Republic to build a Missile Shield defensive system in order to stave off the Iranian and North Korean nuclear threat. Russia perceived that the program was directed against them and thus threatened to build up its military components at its exclave of Kaliningrad (Frye 2021, 171). Further, Russia engaged in a war with Georgia in order to reinstate its control over the border enclaves of South Ossetia and Abkhazia. Although the Georgia government initiated the conflict

## Domestic and Global Security Challenges

in its regions, Russia responded with an overextended military effort to assert control over those two regions within the borders of Georgia. Plans at the NATO Bucharest Summit of 2008 to open its door to possible admission of both Georgia and Ukraine sealed the Putin conclusions about the need to rebuff virtually all Western overtures to and involvement in the region.

## 2014 Russian Takeover of Crimea

Militarization of eastern Ukraine was a predominant feature of the 2014 takeover of Crimea and its immediate aftermath. Russian separatists there fought for control of Odesa, as well as the Luhansk and Donetsk regions. It was clear that Russian soldiers were part of this military operation, but Putin dismissed such charges by saying that the only Russian soldiers there were on leave and taking part on a voluntary level. He had initially denied also that Russian soldiers had moved into Crimea but later admitted that they had landed there and been part of the military effort (Kalb 2015, 19–27). During the crisis that continued on after the Crimea annexation, Russian soldiers mistakenly brought down a Malaysian airline with 300 civilians on board, and the leadership again shoved the blame in another direction by suggesting that the mistaken shooting was probably that of Ukrainian forces. Russia decided to set up a new air base in Belarus to send another message to Ukraine, and they also planned to create another new facility in their own country but on the border with Ukraine. They planned to locate 5,000 troops at each new military base. In August of 2015, the new President Poroshenko summarized that the Russian increased military presence in eastern Ukraine included 500 tanks, 400 artillery systems, and 950 Panzer vehicles (Peterson 2017, 151–52). It is possible that this expansion of military infrastructure and personnel was linked to plans for future engagements in Ukraine as well.

It is also vital to examine diplomatic meetings held in 2014–15, in order to comprehend how nations in the region reacted to the destabilizing events connected with the Russian move into parts of Ukraine. In 2014, months after the spring Crimea acquisition by Russia, NATO held its Wales Summit at which the allies decided to upgrade the defense preparedness of Poland, Estonia, Latvia, and Lithuania by rotating troops from southern Europe to their territory. Importantly, the alliance also set up a Spearhead military force that NATO could dispatch quickly to an emergency area of concern (Peterson 2017, 157). This was in addition to the NATO Response Force that had been part of their planning process for some time. In February 2015, four nations in the region surrounding Ukraine held a summit in Minsk, Belarus. The parties in that discussion included Russia, Ukraine, Germany, and France. They agreed that a pull-back of military forces was the best strategy for all parties involved in the continuing conflict in Ukraine. Ukraine would grant additional autonomy to the two main eastern provinces. The parliament in Kyiv did pass a resolution to do that, but the complication occurred when Ukraine required that such provinces first hold Kyiv-approved elections before that grant of power occurred. Of course, the eastern provinces resisted that requirement (Peterson 2017, 148).

A regional meeting of a very different kind occurred in Moscow on the May 9, 2015, occasion of the 70th anniversary of the end of WWII. This had traditionally been the major Russian holiday, as it was a time to celebrate their lost soldiers as well as their major role in defeating the Nazis. This event and the invitation from Putin to attend it put quite a bit of pressure on East European leaders, for they were troubled and uncertain about going to an event that would place Russia on the center of the stage so soon after observing Moscow's troubling and instigating role in the Crimean conflict. In the end, there was a division among certain leaders, for Czech President Miloš Zeman did choose to take part in the ceremony, as did the Slovak Prime Minister Robert Fico. However, Slovakia's President Andrej Kiska chose to stay home, as after all, each of the East European states had occasion to hold their own commemorations of the end of the war as well.

In the end, the diplomatic meetings merged with the military decisions made in the post-Crimea period in the ambiguity and complexity of their meanings. For Eastern Europe, the key issue was their protection and the evolving role of NATO and the EU in achieving that objective.

## 2022 Russian Invasion of Ukraine

These matters became critical after the February 24, 2022, Russian invasion of Ukraine. As Table 5.2 demonstrates, Russia possessed at the beginning of that war more than four times the active military firepower that Ukraine had under its military command. In terms of the Global Firepower Rank Order, Russia was second only to the United States. Ukraine ranked 22nd but still had higher numbers than did any Eastern European state. Only Poland's rank at 24th

**Table 5.2** Defensive capabilities of Eastern European states, Russia, and Ukraine in 2022.

| Country | Active military manpower | Global firepower rating (0 is perfect) | Global firepower rank order (out of 140) | Up or down movement in last year |
|---|---|---|---|---|
| Russia | 850,000 | 0.0501 | 2 | Up |
| Ukraine | 200,000 | 0.3266 | 22 | Up |
| Poland | 120,000 | 0.4179 | 24 | Same |
| Romania | 67,000 | 0.5938 | 38 | Up |
| Czechia | 26,000 | 0.6161 | 41 | Same |
| Hungary | 23,000 | 0.8633 | 56 | Up |
| Slovakia | 13,000 | 0.9617 | 60 | Same |
| Serbia | 25,000 | 0.9923 | 61 | Up |
| Croatia | 15,000 | 0.9962 | 62 | Up |
| Bulgaria | 30,000 | 1.1071 | 67 | Same |
| Lithuania | 16,000 | 1.7083 | 85 | Same |
| Slovenia | 7,000 | 1.9486 | 86 | Up |
| Latvia | 6,500 | 2.2758 | 94 | Same |
| Moldova | 6,000 | 2.5799 | 105 | Same |
| Estonia | 6,500 | 2.6527 | 108 | Same |
| Albania | 8,000 | 3.0023 | 115 | Down |
| Bosnia-Herz. | 9,000 | 4.0288 | 123 | Same |
| Montenegro | 2,000 | 4.8015 | 131 | Down |
| N. Macedonia | 7,500 | 5.7275 | 134 | Down |
| Kosovo | 3,500 | 13.9136 | 139 | Up |

www.globalfirepower.com, January 23, 2022.

was close to Ukraine. The total number of active military forces in Eastern Europe was 390,500, a figure that was half of Russia's and double that of Ukraine's. It was unlikely that any further Russian provocation could force all the Eastern European countries to merge their militaries for a battle, but their capabilities along with the forces and equipment that NATO had emplaced in the region would make the region a credible balance to Russian military power.

In reacting to the Russian invasion and in preparing to deter future such interventions, NATO held its summer summit in Madrid at the end of June 2022. They announced that high readiness forces would henceforth number over 300,000. They also invited both Sweden and Finland to become formal NATO members, and by that time Turkey had removed its objections, in response to promises about restricting Kurdish extremist groups by other NATO partners as well as by the likely new members. They also passed a new NATO Strategic Concept that, for the first time, mentioned the challenges from China. In that light, several Indo-Pacific partners attended a NATO Summit for the first time, and they included Australia, New Zealand, Japan, and the Republic of Korea. Interestingly, they scheduled their 2023 Summit in Lithuania, one of the Baltic states most threatened by Russia (NATO 2022b).

The "Madrid Summit Declaration" revealed the anger of the NATO leaders at the impulsiveness, irrationality, and brutality of Putin's war on Ukraine. In Point 3 they condemned his war of aggression as well as "Russia's appalling cruelty" in the steps taken to execute it. They reaffirmed in Point 4 their support for Ukrainian President Zelenskyy and the need to keep Ukraine as an independent state. In Point 9, they described a 360-degree military strategy that included the critical components of land, air, maritime, cyber, and space. The alliance will promote more cooperation between host nations and framework nations in areas such as additional collective defense exercises. In Point 15, they also reiterated the need to strengthen and upgrade their partnership with the EU. In light of the Russian aggression, NATO partners promised to provide additional support to vulnerable states including Bosnia-Herzegovina, Georgia, and Moldova (Point 17). They described in Point 18 the significant trilateral memorandum among Turkey, Sweden, and

**Domestic and Global Security Challenges** 133

Finland that offered their traditional "Open Door" to the latter two. In Article 3 of the original Washington Treaty that founded their alliance, leaders had written about the need to strengthen and share defense spending costs, and in Point 19 of the Madrid Summit Declaration, they applied that vision as a very pressing one after the February 2022 Russian invasion of Ukraine. Profoundly, the 2022 invasion led to intensification of existing alliance goals as well as new plans for stronger present and future collective defense policies (NATO 2022a).

The follow-up "NATO 2022 Strategic Concept" carried through on the Declaration in significant ways. In a broad way the Concept sharply and visibly described the Russian Federation as the main threat to the peace and stability of the Euro-Atlantic region. Further, they warned about the emerging strategic partnership between Russia and China. For the first time, they warned that China was a considerable challenge to NATO "interests, security and values." At the minimum, the alliance would try to keep communications open with Russia in hopes of an eventual change in the mindset and policies of their leadership. Notably, the NATO leaders refused to back down at all on their "Open Door" policy of over 70 years towards potential new members. They reaffirmed in a strong way that the partners themselves would decide about new members, and "no third party has a say in this process." If Russia had any interest in violating the territory of official NATO members such as Estonia, Latvia, Lithuania, or Poland, the alliance would promise to defend "every inch" of its members' territory (NATO 2022c). At a minimum, NATO would not back down whatsoever in light of Russia's imperial actions but would instead fuse its traditional convictions with new goals for more extended protection of its members and their region.

## Theoretical Conclusion

Legacy Theory certainly impacted Putin's stated perceptions of the significance of Ukraine and its heritage to Russian history. Russian citations of experiences and events from the tenth century made that clear. Negative legacies from the twentieth century also played a role in the conflict, for Russians bore perceptions of the Munich Pact and Molotov-Ribbentrop Agreement that conflicted with Western views of both matters. Ukraine focused more on legacies from the post-communist era, for their thirty years of state independence had become a heritage that Moscow could only unwind with great difficulty. Alliance Politics Theory was central to the struggle, for the West possessed a thirty-state NATO military alliance that was likely to expand soon to thirty-two members. There were sharply different viewpoints about NATO expansion on both sides as well. From the vantage point of the West, the expanded alliance served several purposes. It was a defensive alliance in case threats emerged from anywhere nearby. After all, Bulgaria and Romania had gained entry to the alliance earlier than expected due to the proximity to the wars in Iraq and Afghanistan. From the Russian perspective, NATO expansion was directed against them, with an eye on restricting their movements in the same way that the alliance did between 1949 and 1991. Balance of Power Theory was a kind of hidden concept behind the whole Russian-Western conflict over the Ukraine War and other matters. NATO's statement of goals after the Russian invasion made it stronger and more unified than it had been in many years. In a sense the situation approximated the years of the early 1990s when President George H. W. Bush and the Americans nearly dominated a unicameral power structure. Soon that yielded to multilateralism with a host of state and non-state actors exercising influence in various regional theaters of the international order. Balance of Power Theory often implied a duality of power centers, but what would be the counterpoint to the West? In Putin's mind, it would be Russian overtures to China coupled with aggressiveness in Russian border areas such as Georgia, Ukraine, and perhaps Moldova. It is unlikely that an equal balance of power would result, and the near universal denunciation of Putin's move into Ukraine undermined any of his hopes to counter NATO, the EU, and American power in a significant way.

# Chapter 6

# THE CLOUD OF COVID-19 AS A GLOBAL PRESSURE ON THE REGION AND ITS INDIVIDUAL STATES, 2020 AND AFTER

*JAMES W. PETERSON*

The spread of the COVID-19 virus was a powerful globalization force that generated national reactions in varying ways within the states of Eastern Europe. Infections were high in all the countries of the region, but the policies taken by the leaders of the various governments were individually related to their own national circumstances and thus quite different from one another. In order to inject clarity into this discussion, there will be three categories of nations under review. The first will be NATO members in the northern half of the region. They include the Baltic states of Estonia, Latvia, and Lithuania as well as the East Central European states of Poland, Hungary, Czech Republic, and Slovakia. A second category includes NATO member states from Southeast Europe. Former Yugoslav republics in this stage of the study include Slovenia, Croatia, Montenegro, and North Macedonia. Additional Balkan states consist of Albania, Bulgaria, and Romania. The third category of countries includes the non-NATO states of Serbia, Kosovo, and Bosnia-Herzegovina. The first two regions differ in the sense that the northern states had traditionally been more economically developed and more politically attuned to democratic procedures than the southern. The third category consists of one state that had been markedly pro-Russian as well as independent of Western alliance pressures and two states whose civil wars still required considerable assistance from NATO and the EU.

## Key Historical Differences

Historically, there have been major differences between the seven political systems that have constituted the Baltics/East Central

Europe in the north and the ten political entities that have made up the Balkans to the south. The first category of states experienced political independence after WWI, and there were democratic outbursts in some of them during communist times, most notably in Poland, Hungary, and Czechoslovakia. In contrast, the Balkan experience with the practice of democracy was a more checkered one. In fact, four of the states were part of the Yugoslav Federation and thus were republics within that semi-imperial unit. The other three were independent, but their experience with democracy was a limited one. Further, there were no democratic rebellions during the Cold War in Bulgaria, Albania, and Romania. Therefore, democratic preparations were more extensive in the northern region than in the southern.

In fact, those divergent historical patterns continued, for the most part, through the first three decades of the post–Cold War era. The Democratic Matrix covers the entire 1900–2019 time frame, and its highest awarded rating was that of a Working Democracy. Four states in the Baltics/East Central Europe received that rating throughout the entire period, and they included the three Baltic states and the Czech Republic. Within the Balkan area, only Slovenia received the label of a Working Democracy. The ranks of the countries in comparison with a broad range of other states were, as well, sharply different. The average ranking of states in the north was a high 35.85, while the comparable rating in the Balkans was a lower 64.28. It is surprising that entry into such a profoundly different world in 1989 did not smooth out systemic differences, especially since a number of scholars in the West in the 1990s declared that "democratic peace" had supplanted Cold War hostilities.

## Impact of COVID-19 on Democratic Ratings

The Democratic Indices focused on ratings during the two years of the COVID-19 crisis, but their findings were somewhat in tune with the above-noted historical differences of the Democracy Matrix over a very extensive period of time. The initial period of the virus did not hamper the democratic ratings of four of the states in the Baltics/East Central Europe, but some negativity about democracy did emerge

# The Cloud of COVID-19

in Estonia, and democratic ratings plummeted in both Poland and Hungary. Within the Balkans, the most notable drops took place in Slovenia, Montenegro, and Albania. Clearly, special political circumstances highlighted both Estonia and Slovenia, as their drops in democratic standings are a surprise in light of their traditional role as the strongest democracies in their regions. However, the general democratic rankings of the two regions did demonstrate sharp differences. On a 100-point scale, the countries of the northern region ranked 70.71, while those states further south received ratings of only 55.71. Thus, regional differences, with some notable exceptions, persisted through the initial two-year period of the virus.

Evidence from the BTI Transformation Index sharpens even more the differences between the two regions. According to the Political Transformation Index, five states in the north enjoyed the highest ratings but only two in the south. Similarly, the Governance Index provides four very good ratings to northern states but none to Balkan states. These tables move a little beyond the matter of democratic standards but reflect values that are often part of the democratic equation.

## Selected Case Studies of Political and Administrative Decisions during the 2020–22 Virus

### East Central European States

In Poland, there were pluses and large minuses in the way in which political and administrative leaders handled the crisis. After the infection became a powerful force, in spring 2020, the government imposed a two-month lockdown. However, for political reasons, the government lifted the restrictions just before the presidential elections. The first round of elections occurred in late June and the presidential run-off on June 12. Due to the lifting of the lockdown, President Duda was able to meet voters in order to strengthen his case for re-election. It was also the case that the central government in Warsaw circumvented the local governments in the implementation of the financial needs to combat the disease. For example, the distribution of financial subsidies for medicine and testing equipment depended on whether the local party in charge was the same as the controlling national party (PiS). Further, personal connections between local and central governmental levels often determined the magnitude of medical equipment provided for localities. When the result was a record number of deaths at the end of the year, a second lockdown went into effect in the last two months of the year (Wójcik and Wratiowski 2021).

The situation in Hungary was equally gloomy, as many steps were taken to preserve power for President Orbán and his Fidesz/Christian Democratic People's Party (KDNP) Party Alliance. From March until June 2020, the government announced that it would govern by decree during the "state of danger." New legislation that included a Criminal Code declared that journalists who articulated false information about the virus would spend some time in prison. In addition, a certain portion of tax receipts collected by municipalities would be refunneled to the central government's Recovery Fund. Renewal of the "state of danger" went into effect as disease rates increased at the end of the year (Végh 2021). As in Poland, any vestige of federalism yielded to central controls in combating COVID-19.

Even though Slovakia ranked high in disease-related death rates in early 2021, they had declared defeat of the pandemic many months earlier in May/June 2020. The central government took over control of the situation in the fall of that year, but they did exclude local municipalities in the decision-making process. By the spring of 2021, the leaders imposed new restrictions that limited the freedom of movement of the population. While the EU had been cautious about purchase of the Sputnik V vaccine, Slovakia went ahead and obtained it at that time (Steuer 2021).

## *Former Yugoslav Republics*

In Slovenia, a new coalition government emerged in 2020, and its main thrust was ideologically center-right with Janez Janša of the Slovenian Democratic Party as the Prime Minister. Their lockdowns often restricted "irregular immigrants" more than they did the regular population. Evidence existed that there was considerable corruption in their efforts to obtain emergency medical equipment. As a result, demonstrations occurred against these governmental abuses of power, and the new government took very hardline stands against them (Lovec 2021).

Croatia experienced similar tensions, but a difference lay in the personal nature of some of the abuses of power. Pandemic restrictions were in place, but many high officials broke them, and that included a visit by President Zoran Milanović to a prohibited private club. In addition, safety rules were relaxed in summer 2020, in part due to the upcoming parliamentary elections. Part of the reason for the exceptions to the tough pandemic restrictions was a concern that they would hurt tourism, a true staple of the Croatian economy (Prelec 2021).

There were several abuses of power in Montenegro following the initial tightening of restrictions. For example, the government introduced criminal proceedings against five private citizens who were identified as having contributed to a sense of panic about the medical crisis. Further, the new laws stated that citizens ordered into 14-day isolation due to the disease should have the right to keep their names private from the rest of the public. However, at one point the government violated this regulation by publishing their names. Steps like that undermined the hatching plans for Montenegro to apply for membership in the EU (Marović 2021).

North Macedonia had the second highest rate of infections in the Balkans, and thus the government instated rule by emergency decree. The restrictions included curfews, limits on gatherings, border closures, and exercise of work and teaching within exclusively online settings. In addition, the government quarantined many expatriates who had moved to the nation. Government restrictions also intensified tensions with the minority Albanian regions, whose infection rates and resistance to lockdown steps were high (Bliznakovski 2021).

## *Southeastern European States*

The Albanian government also ordered a state of emergency as well as a partial lockdown, and there were many who blamed those steps

140 **The Cloud of COVID-19**

for a recession in the fall. Any demonstrators who violated the pandemic regulations were fined in an effort to restrict any sort of civic activism. Even President Ilir Meta organized rallies against Prime Minister Edi Rama for his stern actions (Vurmo 2021).

In Bulgaria, there were urban/rural issues in the governmental responses to the pandemic. The capital city of Sofia received relatively thorough medical care and supplies, but the outlying cities and towns did not. In the summer of 2020, businesses pressured the government to ease the lockdown, but the result was the highest infection rate in Europe by the fall. Subsequently, the government imposed a tough lockdown in November. Tension with Romany communities also took place, for the government set up police checkpoints that did not exist in the rest of the country (Petrov 2021). Clearly, political pressures and the resulting conflicts characterized the difficult situation in Bulgaria.

## Election Outcomes during the Crisis Years

It is also useful to examine the experience of election outcomes and party turnovers during the time of the pandemic. In the region of the Baltics/East Central Europe, five of the seven states held elections for parliament or president, but only in the Czech Republic was there a change in party control. The defeat of Babiš and his party Ano did not center primarily on his handling of the pandemic, but the eventual outcome of the election was a shift in power to Spolu and the new Prime Minister Petr Fiala. In the Balkans there were eight elections and several switches in party control. The party that had governed Bulgaria since 2009 lost, while bargaining over their successor resulted in a new parliamentary coalition. In Montenegro, the 2020 parliamentary elections replaced a party-based governing body with an expert one, a pattern similar to the experience of the Czechs in an earlier decade. A new three-party coalition emerged in Romania in their 2020 parliamentary elections, while the experience in Croatia was somewhat different. The result in Croatia was not a party changeover, but rather the emergence of an SPD president in place of governing by an Independent. Overall, it will take further research to investigate closely the potential effect of the

# The Cloud of COVID-19

virus in undermining support for existing governments in the four, or five, cases of party control changes.

Attention to election results in the three non-NATO/non-EU states is significant as well, for they differed in important ways. Serbia's Alexander Vučić had headed the state since 2012, and his roles had included prime minister as well as president. In fact, the opposition boycotted the 2020 elections, and so his subsequent victory was inevitable. Elections in Bosnia-Herzegovina were unusual in the sense that the Dayton Agreement mandated a three-person presidency, with representatives from the Muslim or Bosniak group, Serbs, and Croatians. In elections for the House of Representatives, voters would choose from those seeking office from the Republika Serbska or from the Federation of Bosnia and Herzegovina that pulled in both Bosniaks and Croatians. The scheduled elections of fall 2022 were somewhat ominous, for Serbs had been calling for the break-up of the federative state, and some Croatians had been lobbying for a Croatian right for their ethnic group to have the only say in choosing their member of the collective presidency (Hitchner 2021).

Probably Kosovo had the most troubled experience with democracy and electoral politics in recent years. Parliamentary elections were held in 2019, and the first-place finish of the opposition party Vetëvendosje led to a fragile coalition with the previously leading party, the Democratic League of Kosovo (LDK). The latter's leader, Albin Kurti, emerged as prime minister, but the coalition collapsed at the end of March 2020, after the LDK filed a no-confidence motion. Kurti continued on as a caretaker prime minister, but all of that disappeared a few months later in June. He had not been successful in forming a government, and so his LDK elected their own Avdullah Hoti as the new prime minister. A central feature of the disagreement within the party was the correct method to cope with COVID-19, and so that issue of the 2020–22 period had a significant impact on their political system. New elections were held in February 2021 and Kurti with the LDK won a landslide victory, and so this undid the results of the 2019 elections. Clearly, Kosovo's drop in democratic ratings was correlated with instability surrounding leadership management of the COVID-19 crisis and the close balance both among the main political parties and among rival leaders within the LDK.

## Theoretical Conclusion

It would be tempting to conclude that Chaos Theory best explains the completely unanticipated advent of COVID-19 on Eastern Europe. After all, there had not been such a devastating health crisis since the 1918 Flu Pandemic. Leaders of the Eastern European states under consideration in this study were completely unprepared for what political decisions should look like in such a new and tumultuous situation. Given the wide range of political responses to include restrictions on the population, postponement of elections, difficulties in transporting needed medical supplies to the entire population, and occasional retaliation against both protestors and minority groups, Chaos Theory is a persuasive one. At the same time, the crisis called for highly imaginative and continuous responses by public managers who presided over public bureaucracies that held responsibility for responding to the changing needs of the general population and key interest groups. Public Management Theory was thereby a galvanizing and centralizing force in organizing these challenging responses. Accordingly, Public Policy Theory is pertinent as well, for its innovative aspects were in high demand in such highly charged times. As leaders thought through their eventual decisions on the specific challenges of COVID-19, policies took on a new look and applicability to very transformed situations.

# Chapter 7

## CONCLUSION: IMPERIALISM, GLOBALIZATION, AND NATIONALISM IN EASTERN EUROPE IN THE TWENTY-FIRST CENTURY

### *JAMES W. PETERSON*

The three dynamic forces that underplay and at times undergird the policy formation process of the states of Eastern Europe each have their separate effects but also are often intertwined. It is interesting and disturbing that imperialism disappeared temporarily after World War I and led many observers and participants to conclude that it would not return. However, it did reappear in the form of Nazism in the 1930s and 1940s as well as in the form of twenty-first-century Russian aggression in its wars with Ukraine. Globalization intensified with the advent of modern computer technology, transportation systems, and an unending multiplicity of communication systems. As such, it generated both a sense of state weakness and a continuing idea of threat to national leaders and their populations. Nationalism in the region was continuously a double-edged sword. On the one hand, it constituted a force to pull together the various groups within the newly freed post-communist states in various ways that made state functioning possible within a complicated region. On the other hand, nationalistic forces often provided the strong hand to pull apart the stitches of the emerging states and at times led to disastrous civil conflicts. It is unclear what the exact relationship is among these three competing forces, but the continuing challenge for the Eastern European systems is to prevent an unholy alliance among them and also to work towards ironing out their intense conflicts to make policy-making a more stable process.

## Imperialism

Imperialism characterized the entire region prior to 1918, and World War I itself broke the backs of four empires that over time had developed fragility and huge weaknesses. By the end of the war, the Austro-Hungarian, German, Russian, and Ottoman empires had fallen apart in their existing forms. For the most part, the peoples that emerged with nation-states had been working towards that new goal under the control of those empires for many decades and were ready for a fresh start. For example, many had rebelled against the Austro-Hungarian Empire and its capital in Vienna in 1848, and that popular set of outbreaks led to a new belief that national autonomy was a possibility. Throughout Europe and even in the United States, that period of history was replete with the unification of states under the banner of nationalism. Both Italian and German unification brought new entities that linked their very disparate regions together. For example, in Germany, Bavaria had a very distinctive culture but was pulled into a new state with regions that were quite different from their own. Many of the East European peoples imitated those movements while still under the imperial controls of Vienna. For example, Czechs developed their own political parties that served in the Austrian legislature. They also substituted the Czech language for German in many cultural settings such as the National Theater that they built themselves and opened in 1881. They had laid the foundation for it in 1868, and the stone arrived from Říp, the location into which its mythic founder Praotec Czech had supposedly first entered the Czech Lands, perhaps in the seventh century. In spite of these nationalist signposts, the overall imperial framework in a weakening form lasted until 1918 in the entire region.

However, the revival of imperialism under Hitler in the early 1930s suffused all of those new national ambitions under a cloud of horror and destruction. In a sense, German intense nationalism spearheaded this form of imperialism, but it temporarily erased many national units that had emerged from World War I in the first years after 1918. The Munich Agreement of 1938 erased Czechoslovakia from the map and divided it into two Nazi-controlled puppets. Poland, which had disappeared from the map

## Conclusion

between the 1790s and 1918, yielded its own political disappearance again after the invasion in 1939. In the end, Hitler's forces took over all of Europe with the exception of Great Britain. Further, they violated the Molotov-Ribbentrop Pact by invading the Soviet Union in a similar but failed effort in 1941. Fortunately, this period of brutal imperialism ended in 1945 with the Allied victory.

Following the Nazi defeat in 1945, there was an assumption that imperialism in its pre–World War I form was dead. However, to many, the decades of Soviet Union control that followed harked back to the imperial forms and controls of the nineteenth century and before. The peoples who existed within it certainly saw it as a new assertion of imperial controls, although Moscow always claimed that participation in regional units such as the Warsaw Treaty Organization was purely voluntary by the nations of Eastern Europe.

Again, optimism reigned after 1989 with a renewed assumption that imperialism would never again reemerge. However, Russian attacks on an independent Ukraine in 2014 but especially in 2022 reminded its Eastern European neighbors that an imperialism that left both nationalism and globalization in its wake or in a ditch had reemerged with a terrible force and many victims. President Putin had bemoaned the implosion of the Soviet Union for many years, and domination again of all or part of Ukraine became an intense but inscrutable goal of his. The capture of Crimea in 2014 was the first step in the process and partly an accident that was due to the Maidan Revolt in Ukraine against the elected Russian ethnic and Russia-leaning leader Viktor Yanukovych in 2010. The February 2022 invasion by Russia was a purposeful expression of a totally outdated imperialism that seemed to be mainly a product of the imagination of Vladimir Putin. The capture of the Donbas that included the Donetsk and Luhansk regions was the ostensible aim, but the attempted invasion of the capital city of Kyiv and the devastating bombing of selected cities all over the country indicated an appetite for much more. Many observers pointed out that such an attempted imperialist power grab had not reared its head since the Nazi efforts of the 1930s and 1940s. Some others pointed out that battlefield conditions, with soldiers in trenches that received

**146**  **Conclusion**

sudden attacks from above, approximated the primitive situation of World War I, in which many died in efforts to extend their trenches forward by inches or feet. The casualty levels were very high and included countless innocents and, sadly, children. Imperialism had returned to the world with devastating effects.

The most powerful analytical explanation for the recurring phenomenon of imperialism is Legacy Theory. The four empires prominent in Eastern Europe left important legacies that did not rest entirely on their control mechanisms to contain the potential nations within them. After the empires collapsed, many of their own national groups remained within the new states, and their coexistence with the new state-based majorities was complicated and many times conflictual. Ottoman Turks remained as a considerable minority in Bulgaria and their status and dreams were uneasy into the early twenty-first century. Similarly, ethnic Germans who remained in Czechoslovakia after 1918 did not all have the freedom that the last Austrian administrator did, who simply handed over the keys to the Castle in Prague, with its administrative offices and museum of St. Wenceslaus, to Czech administrators, walked down to the Prague train station, and took the next train back to Vienna. The Sudeten Germans remained to become a tool of Adolph Hitler and later made a sad trek out of their new country of Czechoslovakia. The legacy of Hitlerism in Eastern Europe was profound as well and convinced the leaders of the newly freed Eastern European states to prevent it from ever dominating their states again. Of course, that is the reason why their forced submission to Moscow after the late 1940s was such an incredible let-down. Leaders of each newly freed nation in the region rejoiced in the chance to restore the national autonomy of 1918 but quickly had to put such hopes aside for the next forty-five years. Legacies played an enormous role after 1989, for each state in Eastern Europe fought hard to establish the autonomy that they remembered as a major achievement of 1918. This time, their hopes to establish better legacies for the future were warranted, although the experiences were a very mixed blessing. Balkan Wars of the 1990s raised all of the old disappointments again, but a number of states in the Baltic area and in East Central Europe were able to maintain the controls and traditions of freer social orders.

# Conclusion

147

What would Russian efforts in 2022 to establish imperial controls over Ukraine or a part of it bode for the future? The answer to that is unclear but must begin with efforts by Russians themselves to establish new legacies about the meaning of their nation that sharply differ from the distorted dreams of Vladimir Putin.

## Globalization

The Western market approach and its liberalism accompaniment became a serious globalization pressure in the region after the 1989 anti-communist revolutions. In this case, the new regimes in Eastern Europe welcomed the pressure as an instrument for moving away from the intense communist-era economic controls. Leaders after 1989 invited Western experts on what capitalist management of the economy could look like, and the new governments worked with them to break up the communist methods of economic control. The Eastern European leaders had a smörgåsbord of choices among Western models, from the open free market with fewer state controls in the United States to the more centralized systems of the Scandinavian states. Some of the new governments such as those in Poland and the Czech Republic opted to make the transition very quickly, and it was a painful process in the short run but very successful in making a relatively fast transition over the long haul. Others such as Bulgaria spread the pain out over an extended period but then took much longer to set up capitalist economies with all their features (Stoyanova 2020). In this case, the globalization pressure was certainly western in origin, and there were few in Eastern Europe who questioned this transition as a necessity.

A globalization pressure that was eastern in its source was clearly the huge refugee flow that began in 2015–16 and then continued on in 2022. There was a sharp difference in the Eastern European receptivity to these two sets of globalization pressures. Antagonism reigned supreme in the first set from the Middle East and Afghanistan, and that had much to do with the "differentness" of the people coming in as well as their violent and terrorism-riddled homelands. East European governments at times erected fences to prevent their entry into the states and at other times resisted EU quotas of refugees, based on the populations of the new host states, for each country in the region as well as in the western part of Europe. However, in 2022, the Eastern Europeans were much more receptive to incoming Ukrainian refugees from their war with Russia. Some saw them as fellow Slavs who had received the same kind of brutal treatment that they had under communist rule. Others such as Poland already had considerable Ukrainian populations, and the people fleeing the war were able to link up and perhaps live with them. Of course, there was also considerable sympathy for the ways in which this war had begun and for the extent of its damage to human beings as well as property. In spite of this contrast in the impact of the two refugee experiences in Eastern Europe, many Middle Eastern people did find homes in the region while quite a few Ukrainians returned home when home cities such as Kyiv settled down somewhat.

In 2020–22 and after, the pandemic became a very different kind of globalization force that damaged all of the Eastern European states, as it had most other countries of the world. The states differed considerably in the degree to which their governments quickly imposed the needed restrictions such as social distancing, masking, and testing when needed. As the virus passed through at least four stages with upward curves in each, it seemed as if leaders were constantly struggling with the question of when to loosen restrictions and when to tighten them up. Elections also were held as scheduled, and the fortunes of the incumbent leaders who were running themselves or leading their parties in parliamentary choices often depended on how they had responded to the infection. The party in control of Hungary for many years won its election, while the Bulgarian party that had governed since 2009 lost. In some states such as the Czech Republic, a turnover took place but ostensibly had little to do with the way in which the incumbent government had managed the COVID-19 crisis. How to handle this tremendous globalization force was thus much more complicated and multifaceted than the questions connected with introducing a liberal capitalist economic order or figuring out how to absorb huge numbers of refugees.

The most useful theory to utilize in analyzing globalization pressures such as these is Public Policy Theory. The governing officials

## Conclusion

who came to power in Eastern Europe in their first democratically held elections usually had little experience in making tough national decisions. Some, such as Wałesa in Poland and Havel in Czechoslovakia/Czech Republic, had been dissidents whose experience had been in managing large anti-government groups. Others in the Balkans had been part of the communist leadership but changed their perspectives and goals once communism disappeared. They possessed governing experience but were more reluctant to embrace radical Western-based economic reforms. Public policy–elected officials were again primarily responsible for deciding how to react to the two noted refugee flows. National officials decided on questions such as whether to build a fence against the refugees or how to respond to the EU request for accepting a quota of them. However, regional and local public officials offered advice and orders to them about the quota issue as well as later about absorbing Ukrainian refugees. In both cases it was the public policy officials at the lower levels of government who bore the responsibility both of where to house the new members of their societies and of what services to provide. Finally, elected decision-makers were the first to bear the brunt of public responses to the virus in 2020 and after. In contrast to the previous two illustrations of globalization, the leaders needed to respond in days or weeks rather than in months or years. Often the nature of their responses dictated the probability of their own political survival!

## Nationalism

Ethnic conflicts and civil war damaged the new nations of the Balkan region in the first decade after the liberation from communist rule. Smaller nationalistic ethnic groups within certain states made nationalism at the state level a nearly impossible goal to achieve, and that caution by the leaders of the country was also partly because communist rule had clearly downplayed the importance of nationalism in favor of the Marxist-Leninist priority on the proletariat. In the Balkans, the nationalist crisis centered on the tragedy in Bosnia-Herzegovina in the 1992–95 period, with deaths from the civil war in the hundreds of thousands. There were nationalist conflicts among the Bosnian Serbs, Albanians, and Croatians. However, the Serbian army from nearby Yugoslavia entered the war as well to fight for the local Serbian effort to dominate Bosnia. In the end, NATO utilized air strikes to bring the nationalist conflict to a halt, and the Dayton Accord that followed was generally a success.

Terrorism also threatened the states of the region after 9/11, and each country took steps to ensure that similar events and tragedies did not erupt on their territory. In several Eastern European nations, their own citizens had gone into Syria and other places in the Middle East to take part in wars there. This was especially true for the states with large Albanian populations, such as Bosnia, Kosovo, Albania, and North Macedonia. There was an eventual need for those states in the region to follow up when the citizens returned to their home countries from the battle zones. Terrorism also appeared in atrocities such as the mass executions at Srebrenica in Bosnia-Herzegovina as well as an attack on an airport in Bulgaria. Kosovo was the site of eventually thwarted plans by terrorists to attack the defensive KFOR troops as well as an athletic team. In addition, the participation of Eastern European states in NATO's operations in Afghanistan was aimed at defeating the terrorism there, but it also cost a considerable number of lives for Poland, Romania, and the Czech Republic. Nation-building became much more problematic for those states whose leaders were partly preoccupied by developing plans to cope with terrorist threats from inside and outside their nations.

The rise of populism was a global phenomenon that had a sizeable impact on Eastern Europe as well. Each country had within it at least one populist political party, and its leaders often pushed nationalism to its extremes. Battles against global organizations like the EU and NATO were often part of these movements, and leaders such as Orbán in Hungary vowed to protect the nation-state and its hopes against many of the responsibilities that it had taken on within those broader organizations. There was certainly a tinge of authoritarianism in many of these populist leaders and minorities, for they were willing to restrict the rights of most minorities within their nation. At times, their discrimination hit regions of

## Conclusion

the country that had not become part of their own movements, as was the case in Poland when the government restricted COVID-19 medical assistance to states and regions that had not voted for the government in the last election. For populists, the democratic norms and practices that had developed in the state since 1989 could easily yield to strong leaders who sacrificed them in strident appeals to the glory of the nation. Many other democracies experienced the same phenomenon, and the existence of populism in all of them made policy-making quite uncertain.

Divergence and Convergence of States Theory is a useful model to help explain these post-communist populist/nationalist challenges to the countries of Eastern Europe. There was a divergence between the states that were afflicted by the Balkan Wars and those in East Central Europe that were not. While Bosnia and Kosovo experienced bitter and difficult civil wars in the 1990s over ethnic minority rights, Czechs and Slovaks peacefully separated during the "Velvet Revolution" of 1993 into two stable democratic states. Terrorism had a convergence impact on the region, as all states wrestled in similar ways with the ensuing challenges out of the fear of terrorist incidents among their peoples. Sharing of information was critical among and between those states, for the terrorist groups definitely worked across state lines and planned attacks in various nations. Populism had both a diverging and converging influence. On the one hand, many of the leaders converged in the kinds of populist statements they made about the future goals of their countries and peoples, and they shared a mistrust of democracy in their preference for personalist leadership. On the other hand, their excessively nationalist ambitions and speeches had a diverging impact, for they aroused the ancient nationalist hatreds and rivalries that had developed over time but especially after state creation at the end of World War I. For example, the shrunken Hungarian state contained persons who still resented the groups that had benefited in new states after their departure from the Hungarian Empire. More contemporaneously, populists at times exhibited a fondness for their alliance with Russia, in spite of the horrors that flowed from the efforts of Moscow to take over parts of Ukraine.

## Theoretical Conclusions

There has been reliance on twelve different theoretical models in analyzing this broad array of information on the history of Eastern Europe. The authors have applied each one of them to a portion of the conclusions of these case studies. Some such as Balance of Power Theory have fitted the globalization pressures to a greater extent, while others such as Realist Theory were more appropriate in explaining the variables of nationalism. Imperialism on the surface may seem less important, but the reemergence of a Russian imperialist thirst and ambition in the twenty-first century makes that again of significance. Chaos Theory is useful, for it reminds the readers of the parallels to Hitlerian imperialism of the 1930s and 1940s, as well as the centuries of control of the region by four empires prior to 1918. How could nations outside the imperial borders of each setting respond with appropriate and effective policies? When chaos reigned supreme for a long time, capable and responsive policy-making was difficult to achieve.

In the end, three of the twelve models bore the most power to make situations and solutions more clear and more possible. Legacy Theory helps understand the nature of imperialism, for there have been powerful images from past empires that help to understand current ones. Public Policy Theory is most helpful in understanding potential reactions by state leaders to the constant hum of globalization pressures, for they cannot ignore such factors that intrude on their domestic priorities. Divergence and Convergence of States Theory can elucidate the various components of nationalism and help in predicting whether states in Eastern Europe will end up making very similar or quite different decisions. These three theories also blend together in certain ways. Legacies can set the stage for public policy-making in many settings. Policy-making creates new legacies that can impact and absorb both national and global currents. States will converge and diverge over time in the kinds of policies they make in crises of nationalism and globalism, and all of this contributes to the legacies they will pass on to future generations.

# Bibliography

Alcantara, Chris. "46 Years of Terrorist Attacks in Europe, Visualized: 1970–2016." *The Washington Post*, July 4, 2022.

Anderson, James and Liam O'Dowd. "Borders, Border Regions, and Territoriality: Contradictory Meanings, Changing Significance." *Regional Studies* 33, no 7 (1999): 593–604.

Assembly-Kosovo. *Constitution of the Republic of Kosovo*. October 23, 2008. http://www.assembly-kosovo.org/.

Banac, Ivo. *The National Question in Yugoslavia. Origins, History, Politics.* Ithaca: Cornell University Press, 1992.

Barany, Zoltan. "The Military and Security Legacies of Communism." In *The Legacies of Communism in Eastern Europe*, edited by Zoltan Barany and Ivan Volgyes, 101–11. Baltimore: The Johns Hopkins University Press, 1995.

Baskin, Mark and Paula Pickering. "Former Yugoslavia and Its Successors." In *Central & East European Politics: From Communism to Democracy*, edited by Sharon L. Wolchik and Jane L. Curry, 281–315. New York: Rowman & Littlefield Publishers, Inc., 2008.

Baten, Jorg and Mikołaj Szołtysek. "The Human Capital of Central-Eastern and Eastern Europe in European Perspective." MPIDR Working Paper 2012-002. Max-Planck-Institut für Demografi Sche Forschung, Rostock, January 2012. https://www.demogr.mpg.de/papers/working/wp-2012-002.pdf, accessed June 27, 2022.

BBC NEWS. "How Many Ukrainian Refugees Are There and Where Have They Gone?" July 4, 2022.

Bell, David. *The First Total War. Napoleon's Europe and the Birth of Warfare as We Know It.* Boston and New York: Mariner Books, 2008.

Bell, John D. "Bulgaria." In *Developments in East European Politics*, edited by Stephen White, Judy Batt, and Paul D. Lewis, 83–97. Durham: Duke University Press, 1993.

Bliznakowski, Jovan. "North Macedonia: Executive Summary." In *Democracy Indices of Freedom House and Polity 2020–21.* 2021. https://freedomhouse.org/country/north-macedonia/nations-transit/2022.

Brainerd, Elizabeth. "Human Development in Eastern Europe and the CIS Since 1990." In *Human Development Research Paper 2010/16.* United

Nations Development Program, 2010. https://hdr.undp.org/content/human-development-eastern-europe-and-cis-1990, accessed August 16, 2022.

"BTI Transformation Index." 2021. https://bti-project.org/en/?

Carpenter, Ted Galen. *Cato Institute*. December 16, 2015. https://www.cato.org/sites/cato.org/files/pubs/pdf/annual_report-2015.pdf.

Cohen, Leonard J.. *Broken Bonds: The Disintegration of Yugoslavia*. Boulder: Westview Press, 1993.

Connelly, John. *From Peoples Into Nations. A History of Eastern Europe*. Princeton: Princeton University Press, 2020.

Csergo, Zsuzsa. "Ethnicity, Nationalism, and the Expansion of Democracy." In *Central & East European Politics: From Communism to Democracy*, edited by Sharon L. Wolchik and Jane L. Curry, 87–111. New York: Rowman & Littlefield Publishers, Inc, 2008.

Davis, Mike. *Late Victorian Holocausts: El Niño Famines and the Making of the Third World*. London: Verso, 2001.

Democracy Indices of Freedom House and Polity 2020–21. "Countries and Territories." 2021. https://freedomhouse.org/report/freedom-world/2021/democracy-under-siege.

Democracy Matrix DeMax Version 3 (1900–2019). Univeritäts Würzburg, 2019. https://www.democracymatrix.com/.

Dimitrievska, Valentina. "Rooting Out Corruption Proves a Tough Job in North Macedonia." *BNE Intellinews*, 2021. https://www.intellinews.com/rooting-out-corruption-proves-a-tough-job-in-north-macedonia-222530/, accessed August 28, 2022.

Dominique, Monika Rębata. "Eastern Europe Welcomes Some Refugees, Not Others. Is it Only Racism?" *Christian Science Monitor*, March 24, 2022.

Eberstadt, Nicholas. "Demographic Shocks in Eastern Germany, 1989–93." *Europe-Asia Studies* 46, no. 3 (1994): 519–33.

Eberstadt, Nicholas. "The Enigma of Russian Mortality." *Current History* 109, no. 729 (2010): 288–94.

Engels, Friedrich. *The Condition of the Working Class in England (Oxford World's Classics)*. Oxford: Oxford University Press, 2009 [1844].

"Europe: Self-Strangulation; Latvia and Russia." *The Economist* 367, no. 8327 (2003): 42.

Fogel, Robert. *The Escape from Hunger and Premature Death 1700–2100: Europe, America, and the Third World*. Cambridge and New York: Cambridge University Press, 2004.

Freedom House. "Democracy Is Under Attack Across Central and Eastern Europe and Central Asia." April 28, 2021. https://emerging-europe.com/news/democracy-is-under-attack-across-central-and-eastern-europe-and-central-asia/

Frye, Timothy. *Weak Strongman: The Limits of Power in Putin's Russia*. Princeton: Princeton University Press, 2021.

# Bibliography

Giddens, Anthony. *The Constitution of Society. Outline of the Theory of Structuration*. Berkeley and London: Berkeley University Press, 1984.

Gille, Zsuzsa. "Introduction: From Comparison to Relationality." *Slavic Review* 76, no. 2 (2017): 285–90.

Greenfeld, Liah. *Nationalism. Five Roads to Modernity*. Cambridge, MA and London: Harvard University Press, 1992.

Hardt, Michael and Anton Negri. *Empire*. Cambridge, MA and London: Harvard University Press, 2000.

Havel, Vaclav and John Keane. *The Power of the Powerless. Citizens Against the State in Central and Eastern Europe*. Abingon: Routledge, 1985.

Havrylyshyn, Oleh, Xiaofan Meng, and Marian L. Tupy. "25 Years of Reforms in Ex-Communist Countries: Fast and Extensive Reforms Led to Higher Growth and More Political Freedom." *Cato Policy Institute Papers, no. 795*, July 12, 2016. https://www.cato.org/policy-analysis/25-years-reforms-ex-communist-countries-fast-extensive-reforms-led-higher-growth#, accessed August 14, 2022.

Heilbroner, Robert. *The Nature and Logic of Capitalism*. New York: W.W. Norton and Company, 1986.

Hendrickson, Alan K. "Distance and Foreign Policy: A Political Geography Approach." *International Political Science Review* 23, no. 4 (2002): 437–66.

Hendrickson, Ryan C. *Diplomacy and War at NATO: The Secretary General and Military Action After the Cold War*. Columbia: The University of Missouri Press, 2006.

Hill, Carolyn J. and Lawrence E. Lynn Jr. *Public Management: Thinking and Acting in Three Dimensions 2e*. Los Angeles: Sage/CQ Press, 2016.

Hitchner, R. Bruce. "The Time for Electoral Reform in Bosnia and Herzegovina Is Now." *Balkan Insight*, October 27, 2022.

Huntington, Samuel P. *The Clash of Civilizations and the Remaking of the New World Order*. London: Simon and Schuster, 1997.

Hupchick, Dennis P. *Conflict and Chaos in Eastern Europe*. New York: St. Martin's Press, 1995.

Jackael, Eberhard. *Hitler's Worldview: A Blueprint for Power*. Cambridge, MA: Harvard University Press, 1981.

Jentleson, Bruce W. *American Foreign Policy: The Dynamics of Choice in the 21st Century*, 3rd ed. New York: W.W. Norton & Company, 2007.

Jowitt, Ken. *The New World Disorder: The Leninist Extinction*. Berkeley: California University Press, 1992.

Judson, Pieter. "Austria-Hungary." In *International Encyclopedia of WW1 Online*. 2021. https://encyclopedia.1914-1918-online.net/article/austria-hungary, accessed June 27, 2022.

Kalb, Marvin. *Imperial Gamble: Putin, Ukraine, and the New Cold War*. Washington, DC: Brookings Institution Press, 2015.

Kelly, Robert E. "Security Theory in the 'New Regionalism'." *International Studies Review* 9, no. 2 (2007): 197–229.

# Bibliography

Keohane, Robert and Joseph Nye. "Introduction." In *Governance in the Globalizing World*, edited by Jospeh Nye and Phillip Donahue, 1–42. Santa Monica: Brookings Institution Press, 2000.

Konrad, Gyorgy. *Anti-Politics*. San Diego: Harcourt, 1984.

Kovrig, Bennett. "Marginality Reinforced." In *The Legacies of Communism in Eastern Europe*, edited by Zoltan Barany and Ivan Volgyes, 23–41. Baltimore: The Johns Hopkins University Press, 1995.

Kraft, Michael E. and Scott R. Furlong. *Public Policy: Politics, Analysis, and Alternatives*, 4th ed. Los Angeles: Sage/CQ Press, 2013.

Krastev, Ivan. "The Refugee Crisis and the Return of the East-West Divide in Europe." *Slavic Review* 76, no. 2 (2017): 291–6.

Lenin, V. *Polnoe Sobranie Sochinenii*, 5th ed. Moscow, 1975–9, Vol. 36, 15–16.

Lovec, Marko. "Slovenia: Executive Summary." In *Democracy Indices of Freedom House and Polity 2020–21*. 2021. https://freedomhouse.org/country/slovenia/freedom-world/2023.

Lubecki, Jacek and James W. Peterson, eds. *Defending Eastern Europe: The Defense Policies of New NATO and EU Member States*. Manchester: Manchester University Press, 2021.

Maddison, Angus. *The World Economy. Volume 1. The Millennial Perspective*. London and New York: OECD, 2006.

Maddison Project. "Maddison Project Database. Regional Data." 2020. https://www.rug.nl/ggdc/historicaldevelopment/maddison/releases/maddison-project-database-2020, accessed July 31, 2022.

Magyar, Bálint. *Post-Communist Mafia State: The Case of Hungary*. Budapest: Central European University Press, 2016.

Marović, Jovana. "Montenegro: Executive Summary." In *Democracy Indices of Freedom House and Polity 2020–21*. 2021. https://freedomhouse.org/country/montenegro/freedom-world/2023.

Mazower, Mark. *Hitler's Empire. How the Nazis Ruled Europe*. New York: Viking Press, 2008.

Michta, Andrew W. *The Limits of Alliance: The United States, NATO, and the EU In North and Central Europe*. New York: Rowman & Littlefield Publishers, 2006.

Migration and Asylum in Central and Eastern Europe. European Parliament Working Paper. Directorate General for Research, 1998.

Minakov, Mykhailo. "Eastern Europe's Authoritarian Belt in Crisis." *Wilson Center*, October 6, 2020.

NATO. "Madrid Summit Declaration." June 29, 2022a. https://www.nato.int/cps/en/natohq/official_texts_196951.htm, accessed March 22, 2023.

NATO. "Madrid Summit Ends with Far-Reaching Decisions to Transform NATO." June 30, 2022b. https://www.nato.int/cps/en/natohq/news_197574.htm#:~:text=The%20NATO%20Summit%20in%20Madrid,transform%20and%20strengthen%20the%20Alliance., accessed March 22, 2023.

## Bibliography

NATO. "NATO 2022 Strategic Concept." June 30, 2022c. https://www.nato.int/cps/en/natohq/topics_210907.htm?, accessed March 22, 2023.

NATO. "NATO's Military Presence in the East of the Alliance." July 8, 2022d. https://www.nato.int/cps/en/natohq/topics_136388.htm#:~:text=An%20important%20component%20of%20NATO's,%2C%20Poland%2C%20Romania%20and%20Slovakia, accessed March 22, 2023.

O'Flynn, Kevin. "Baltic Grudge Match." *Newsweek*, Atlantic Edition September 12, 2005, 45.

Persson, Gunnar Karl. *An Economic History of Europe. Knowledge, Institutions and Growth, 600 to the Present.* Cambridge and New York: Cambridge University Press, 2010.

Peterson, James W. *NATO and Terrorism: Organizational Expansion and Mission Transformation.* New York: Continuum, 2011.

Peterson, James W. *Building a Framework of Security for Southeast Europe and The Black Sea Region: A Challenge Facing NATO.* New York: The Edwin Mellen Press, 2013.

Peterson, James W. *Russian - American Relations in the Post-Cold War World.* Manchester: Manchester University Press, 2017.

Peterson, James W. and Sarah Kuck. "Political Science and Territorial Borders." *Review of History and Political Science* 5, no. 1 (2017): 1–11.

Peterson, James W. and Jacek Lubecki. *Defense Policies of East-Central European Countries After 1989: Creating Stability in a Time of Uncertainty.* Manchester: Manchester University Press, 2019.

Petrov, Angel. "Bulgaria: Executive Summary." In *Democracy Indices of Freedom House and Polity 2020–21.* 2021. https://freedomhouse.org/country/bulgaria/freedom-world/2023.

Polanyi, Karl. *The Great Transformation. The Political and Economic Origins of Our Time.* Boston: Beacon Press, 2001 [1944].

Prelec, Tena. "Croatia: Executive Summary." In *Democracy Indices of Freedom House and Polity 2020–21.* 2021. https://freedomhouse.org/country/croatia/freedom-world/2023.

Ramet, Sabrina. *Nationalism and Federalism in Yugoslavia 1962–1992.* Bloomington: Indiana University Press, 1992.

Rosdolsky, Roman. *Engels and the 'Nonhistoric' Peoples: The National Question in the Revolution of 1848.* Glasgow: Critique, 1987.

Roskin, Michael G. *The Birth of East Europe*, 4th ed. Upper Saddle River: Prentice-Hall, 2002.

Rothschild, Joseph. *East Central Europe Between the Two World Wars (History of East Central Europe Vol. IX).* New York: Columbia University Press, 1974.

Sachs, Andreas, Claudia Funke, Phillip Krezuer, and Johann Weiss. "Globalization Report 2020." *Berteslmann Stiftung*, 2020a. https://www.bertelsmann-stiftung.de/en/publications/publication/did/globalization report-2020-all-1, accessed August 16, 2022.

## Bibliography

Sachs, Andreas, Claudia Funke, Phillip Krezuer, and Johann Weiss. "Globalization Report: Snippets from Eastern Europe." *Berteslman Stiftung*, 2020b. https://globaleurope.eu/globalization/globalization-report-2020-snippets-from-eastern-europe/, accessed August 16, 2022.

Shkilnyk, Anastasia. *A Poison Stronger than Love: The Destruction of an Ojibwa Community*. Cambridge: Yale University Press, 1985.

Steiner, Zara. *The Lights that Failed: European International History 1919–1933 (Oxford History of Modern Europe)*. Oxford: Oxford University Press, 2007.

Štěpanovský, Jiří. "Mezinárodní Aspekty Nezávislosti Kosova." *Mezinárodní Politika* XXXII, no. 3 (2008): 18–22.

Steuer, M. *Slovakia's Democracy and the COVID-19 Pandemic: When Executive Communication Fails*. March 9, 2021. Retrieved September 2021, from Verfassungsblog https://verfassungsblog.de/slovakias-democracy-and-the-covid-19-pandemic-when-executive-communication-fails/.

Stevens, Stuart. *It Was All a Lie: How the Republican Party Became Donald Trump*. New York: Knopf, 2020.

Stillman, Richard, II. *The American Bureaucracy: The Case of Modern Government*, 3rd ed. Belmont: Thomson/Wadsworth, 2004.

Stoyanova, Veronika. "Bulgaria's Unending Transition to Capitalism." *Jacobin*, November 15, 2020.

Tooze, Adam. *The Deluge. The Great War, America and the Remaking of the European Order*. New York: Viking, 2014.

*U.S. Department of State*. "Country Reports on Terrorism 2019." https://www.state.gov/country-reports-on-terrorism-2/.

Végh, Zsuzsanna. "Hungary: Executive Summary." In *Democracy Indices of Freedom House and Polity 2020–21*. 2021. https://freedomhouse.org/country/hungary/freedom-world/2023.

Vicent, David. *The Rise of Mass Literacy. Reading and Writing in Modern Europe*. Oxford and Malden: Blackwell Publishers – Polity, 2000.

Volgyes, Ivan. "The Legacies of Communism: An Introductory Essay." In *The Legacies of Communism in Eastern Europe*, edited by Zoltan Barany and Ivan Volgyes, 1–19. Baltimore: The Johns Hopkins University Press, 1995.

Vurmo, Gjergji. "Albania: Executive Summary." In *Democracy Indices of Freedom House and Polity 2020–21*. 2021. https://freedomhouse.org/country/albania/freedom-world/2023.

Warren, Keith, Cynthia Franklin, and Calvin L. Streeter. "New Directions in Systems Theory: Chaos and Complexity." *Social Work* 43, no. 4 (1998): 357–72.

White, Stephen and Margot Light. "The Russian Elite Perspective on European Relations." In *Russia and Europe in the Twenty-First Century: An Uneasy Partnership*, edited by Jackie Gower and Graham Timmins, 41–56. New York: Anthem Press, 2007.

*Wikipedia*. "Coalition Casualties in Afghanistan." 2022a. https://en.wikipedia.org/wiki/Coalition.

## Bibliography

*Wikipedia.* "Islamic Terrorism in Europe." 2022b. https://en.wikipedia.org/wiki/Islamic_terrorism_in_Europe.

*Wikipedia.* "Terrorism in Europe." 2022c. https://en.wikipedia.org/wiki/Terrorism_in_Europe.

Wojcik, Anna and Miłosz Wratiowski. "Poland: Executive Summary." In *Democracy Indices of Freedom House and Polity 2020–21.* 2021. https://freedomhouse.org/country/poland/freedom-world/2023.

# Index

Afghanistan, 104, 106–8, 114, 116–17, 119, 127, 134, 147, 150
Albania, 25, 49, 51–2, 56–7, 61, 63–4, 71–2, 74–5, 77, 80, 86–7, 90, 101, 114, 117, 119–21, 131, 135–7
Albanians, 18, 59, 67–8, 98, 100–1, 118–20, 150
alliance, 7, 11, 20, 22, 29–30, 42, 44–5, 52, 65, 81–2, 88, 94, 108, 124, 130, 132–4, 151
anti-globalization, 2, 49
anti-liberal parties, 83–4
anti-liberalism, 69–92
Arab Spring, 102, 108
Austria-Hungary, 22–5, 27–9
Austro-Hungarian Empire, 5, 15, 24, 26, 29–30, 35, 37, 144
authoritarian leaders, 89, 121
authoritarianism, 8, 24, 36, 38, 41–2, 78, 103, 116, 121, 150
Axis powers, 20, 42, 51

Balkan countries, 71, 75, 113, 137
Balkan Wars, 6, 8, 10, 96, 117, 119, 146, 151
Balkans, 2, 28–9, 32, 35, 61, 98–9, 115, 120, 136–7, 139–40, 149
Baltic countries, 56, 70, 72, 74, 78–80, 90
Baltic nations, 18, 29
Baltic states, 6–7, 45, 95, 101, 105, 132, 136
Belarus, 5, 21, 29, 43, 71, 73–4, 77, 87, 105, 111, 127, 129–30
Belarusians, 18, 31, 37, 56
borders, 4, 25, 30, 94, 103, 107–8, 110, 117, 120, 124, 129

Bosnia, 15, 18, 23, 25, 27, 48, 66–8, 71–2, 77, 80–1, 85–6, 96–9, 101, 109, 118, 150–1
Bosnia-Herzegovina, 15, 18, 24 11, 68, 85–7, 90, 93, 96, 98, 103, 114–15, 117–20, 132, 135, 141, 149–50
Bosniaks, 66, 68, 141
Bosnian Serbs, 67, 85, 96–7, 117–19, 150
Bosnians, 18, 24, 31, 59, 97, 100
boundaries, 2, 20, 22–3, 28–9, 56–7
Bulgaria, 26–7, 29–31, 40–2, 45–7, 49, 57–8, 61, 65, 67, 71–2, 74–7, 80, 86–7, 89, 98–9, 102–3, 105–6, 131, 134–6, 140, 146–7, 150
Bulgarians, 18, 24, 27–8, 32, 39, 102, 120

capitalism, 5, 36, 50, 53–5, 69–70, 72, 76–7
Ceaușescu, Nikolae, 54, 63
Chaos Theory, 104, 112, 142, 152
China, 7, 52, 54, 78, 90, 106, 126, 132–4
class oppression, 19, 50–1
colonialism, 13, 17, 28, 44, 50
colonization, 91
communism, 2, 15, 49–50, 52–3, 55, 59–60, 62, 64–5, 69, 75–6, 98, 109, 121, 149
communist Eastern Europe, 56, 58
Communist Party, 38, 51, 58–61, 63
communist: period, 10, 55, 116; regimes, 58–9, 63; communist, 61, 148–9; communist, 52, 54, 57, 69
conflict: ethnic, 93, 103, 149; ethno-secessionist, 65

# Index

convergence theory, 4, 9–10
corruption, 26, 36, 62, 76, 85–6, 90, 139
Council for Mutual Economic Assistance (CMEA), 10
COVID-19, 135–6, 138–42
Crimea, 7, 94, 102, 123–5, 128–9, 145; annexed, 122–124, 129; conflict, 130
Crimean War, 14
Croat-Muslim Federation, 96
Croatia, 19, 47, 66–8, 71, 74, 76, 79–80, 87, 89, 96, 108, 115, 117, 119, 131, 135, 139–40
Croatians, 18, 24, 31, 39, 47, 59, 68, 85, 89. 96, 141, 150
crypto-nationalism, 79
Csurka, István, 79
Czech Lands, 21, 144
Czech Republic, 5, 8, 11, 71–2, 74–8, 80, 87, 89, 94, 99, 105, 109, 111, 115, 117, 128, 135–6, 140, 147–8, 150
Czechia, 22–3, 131
Czechoslovak democracy, 38–9
Czechoslovakia, 10, 20, 22, 24, 30–1, 39, 42, 44–5, 56–61, 63, 65, 75, 136, 146; independent, 21; restored unified, 59
Czechs, 18, 22–3, 28, 31, 38, 48, 56, 59, 140, 144, 151

de-globalization, 34, 43; democracy 19, 26, 35, 37, 76, 82, 122, 136–7, 141, 151; illiberal 3, 88, 121
Democratic Party for Macedonian National Unity, 86
development, 16, 23, 26, 53, 63, 69–70, 73–4, 77–8, 113, 122
Donbas region, 125
Donetsk and Luhansk regions, 145
Donetsk region, 129

East Central Europe, 2, 13, 63, 116, 146, 151
East Germany, 53, 57, 63, 65, 76
economic development, 13, 53, 70, 75, 78
economic growth, 53, 62, 70, 77, 80, 109

economic system, global, 55, 69
economy, capitalist, 54, 147
education, 5, 110–11
elections, 8, 35, 38–9, 76, 79–80, 87–9, 122, 128, 137, 140–2, 148–9, 151
empires, 1–2, 8–10, 13–68, 144, 146, 152; multinational, 3, 45, 49
Engels, Friedrich, 18, 50, 72
England, 13–14, 20, 30, 34
ethnic cleansing, 25, 28, 32, 45, 117–18
ethnic groups, 4, 93, 96, 98, 103, 124, 141
EUFOR (European Union Force), 98, 118
Euro-Atlantic region, 133
European Security and Defense Policy (ESDP), 99
European Union, 3, 48, 70, 89, 94, 115

fascism, 42
fascists, 2–3, 7, 36, 38, 41–2, 48, 59
Federation of Bosnia and Herzegovina, 85, 141
Fidesz, 80, 88, 138
Fidesz-KDNP, 88
Finland, 126, 132–3
former Yugoslavia, 25, 47–8, 66–7, 71–2, 74, 79–80, 103, 106; countries of, 71, 75
France, 14, 20, 25, 30, 33–4, 44, 84, 114, 130
free elections, 35–6, 41, 65, 76
freedom, 34–5, 54, 138, 146
Freedom House, 121–2

generations, 69, 152
genocidal, 19, 30, 35
genocidal intentions, 48
genocide, 32, 46; deliberate, 44; mass, 48
Georgia, 102, 125, 128–9, 132, 134
Georgian war, 7
German empire in Eastern Europe, 49
German expansion in Eastern Europe, 44
German nation-state, 43
Germans, 5, 22, 30, 37–8, 40, 43–4, 46, 48–9, 57–8, 107, 126, 144

## Index

Germany, 25, 29–31, 33, 35–7, 39, 42, 44–9, 74, 106–7, 110–11, 121, 130, 144
Giddens, Anthony, 17
Gierek, Edward, 61
globalism, 1–3, 152
globalization, 1–5, 8–9, 13–68, 77–8, 90–1, 104, 107, 143, 145, 147, 149
globalization force, 3, 5, 8–9, 14, 55, 104, 106, 135, 148
Gold Standard, 33–4
government 5, 39–41, 62, 67, 88, 90, 102, 104, 114, 120, 135, 137–41, 148–9, 151
Great Britain, 25, 33, 44–6, 145
Great Depression, 31, 33, 40–1, 43
Great Recession, 78–80

Habsburg Empire, 15, 18, 22, 74
Herzegovina, 24, 68, 81, 85, 87, 141
historic nations, 18, 21
Hitler, 2, 30, 33, 43–5, 48–9, 124, 144
Hitlerian imperialism, 152
Hitlerism, 146
Hitler's vision, 30, 43
Holocaust, 47
Hungarian Kingdom, 18–20, 23–4
Hungarian minorities, 57, 63, 76
Hungarian nation-state, 19
Hungarian nationalism, 19–20, 27
Hungarian revisionism, 2, 20
Hungarian state, 20
Hungarians, 18–19, 23, 30, 38, 42, 56, 58, 79–80, 89, 106, 111
Hungary, 10–11, 20, 26, 28, 30–2, 35, 41–2, 45–7, 57–8, 61–3, 65, 71–2, 74–7, 79–80, 85–9, 91, 98–9, 106–9, 111, 121–2, 135–8, 148, 150

ideology, 2–3, 43, 49, 65
illiberal, 84–5, 90
imperial controls, 60, 91, 144–5, 147
imperialism, 1–4, 9, 29, 43, 48, 50, 60, 64, 143–6, 152
imperialism and nationalism, 3, 29, 50
independence, 2, 5, 10, 15, 19–20, 22–3, 26, 28, 32, 36, 66, 93, 100, 124
India, 44, 91, 106

instability, 7, 40, 55, 57, 141
institutions, 14, 31, 52, 56, 60, 66, 73, 80, 91, 117; economic 33, 70, 74; political 37, 77, 103
integration, 33, 75, 78, 80, 83
interests, 4, 18, 128, 133
International Monetary Fund (IMF), 69–70, 79
interventions, 25, 126, 132
interwar period, 34, 38, 41, 64
Iliescu, Ion, 79, 86
Iraq, 7, 104, 106, 108, 114, 120, 134
ISIS, 6, 12, 108, 113, 120
Islamized Slavs, 18, 21, 24
Israel, 78, 121
Italy, 25, 45, 47–8, 84, 111

Jews, 26, 37, 46–8, 58
Jugoslovenska Narodna Armija (JNA), 66–67
Justice Party, 76, 88, 121

Kaczyński, Jaroslaw, 109
Kaliningrad, 7, 94–5, 123, 126, 128
Kosovo Albanians, 67, 121
Kosovo Force (KFOR), 67, 99, 119
Kosovo, 99, 101
Krajina, 27, 48, 67–8
Kyrgyzstan, 127

land bridge, 102, 125
languages, 16–17, 24, 94, 101, 111, 128
Latvia, 21, 30, 36–7, 71, 75, 77, 87, 94–5, 98–9, 117, 123, 130–1, 133, 135
LDK (League of Kosovo), 141–2
leaders, 5, 7, 21, 36, 44, 100, 107, 109, 112–14, 117, 121–2, 124, 130, 133, 135, 138, 142, 146–51
leadership, 11, 80, 84, 95–6, 109, 115, 128–9, 133
League of Kosovo *see* LDK
Lebensraum, 43, 46
legacies, 10, 17–18, 37, 72, 74–5, 103, 134, 146, 152
Legacy Theory, 4, 9–10, 93, 103, 123, 133, 146, 152
Lenin, 50–1, 53, 55

# Index

liberal democracies, 23, 31, 35, 37–8, 40–1, 73

liberalism, 5, 13, 17, 19, 22, 31, 39–40, 42–3, 52–3, 57, 63, 67, 69, 76–9, 90; conservative 28, 33; democratic 20, 22, 31; economic 4–5

Lithuania, 21, 30, 37, 42, 71–2, 75–7, 87, 89, 94–5, 99, 105, 117, 123, 126, 130–3, 135

lockdown, 137–8, 140

logic of nationalism, 3, 34, 36

Macedonia, 6, 24–5, 66, 68, 71, 81, 86, 101, 103, 108–9, 115, 119, 121, 131; civil war in, 93, 101

Macedonian government, 67

Macedonians, 18, 24, 28, 31, 39, 59

Maddison Project, 32, 53–4, 69

Madrid Summit Declaration, 132–3

mafia-states, 76

Magyar, Bálint, 57, 76, 85

Marx, Karl, 50–1

Marxism-Leninism, 3, 15, 53, 60

Marxist-Leninist nation-state, 51

mass killings, 25, 28, 46, 49, 66, 73

massacres, 32, 48, 115

migrants, 105–9, 111

migration, 6, 106, 108

militarism, 13, 62–3, 65

military, 13, 29, 38, 51, 63, 94, 97, 115, 125, 132

military alliance, 98, 125

Milošević, Slobodan, 79, 99

minorities, 4, 17, 30, 38, 103, 123, 150

modernity, 18, 28, 61; technological 53, 55

modernization: cultural, 14; economic, 15–16; outward, 90; social, 14, 53

Moldova, 8, 15, 18, 65, 74–7, 80, 86–7, 89–90, 93, 101–2, 110–11, 131–2, 134

Molotov-Ribbentrop Agreement, 134

Montenegro, 25, 27, 68, 71, 77, 80, 82, 87, 117, 131, 135, 137, 139–40

Moscow, 7, 60, 63, 94, 124, 126, 130, 134, 145–6, 151

movements, 24, 41, 94, 98, 105–6, 110, 131, 134, 138, 144, 150–1

multinational states, 1, 31, 53, 59

Muslim-majority state, 114

Muslims, 85, 96–7, 115, 118, 141

nation-states, 3, 5–6, 16, 29, 43, 99, 113, 144, 150

nationalism, 1–6, 8–11, 13–68, 76, 85, 89, 91, 98, 101–3, 107, 143–5, 149, 152; anti-German, 58; ethnic, 95; modern, 9, 13–14, 19; subordinate, 17

nationalism and globalization, 3, 8–9, 91, 145

nationalist, 75–6, 81–2, 85, 89

nationalist conflicts, 80, 150

nations, 3–4, 8, 11–12, 21–2, 27–8, 31, 34, 43, 50–1, 53, 67–8, 93, 98, 100, 128–30, 135, 139, 145, 147, 150–2

NATO (North Atlantic Treaty Organization), 7, 25, 56, 67, 74, 94, 96–9, 110, 114–15, 117, 119, 125–7, 129–30, 132–3, 135, 150

NATO: key alliance, 123; members of, 7, 58, 77, 116, 135

NATO air attack on Serbian positions, 99

NATO alliance, 123

NATO expansion, 134

NATO involvement, 98, 119

NATO leaders, 132–3

NATO member states, 135

NATO operation, 97, 99

NATO partners, 126, 132

NATO Partnership for Peace Plan, 10

NATO Program, 125

NATO Response Force, 130

NATO's statement of goals, 134

Nazi Empire, 5, 44

Nazi Germany, 5, 20, 40, 42, 44–7, 49, 51, 58

Nazis, 42, 44, 47–8, 58, 130

Nazism, 2, 49, 125, 143

Nordstream pipeline, 123, 126

North Atlantic Treaty Organization see NATO

North Macedonia, 77, 80, 86–7, 101, 120, 135, 139, 150

**164**        **Index**

Operation Allied Force (OAF), 99
Orbán, Viktor, 3, 88, 91, 108, 121, 150
Ottoman Empire, 13, 15–16, 18, 21,
 24–25, 27–30, 35, 90, 102, 144

Paris Peace Treaty, 20, 26
parliamentary elections, 40–1, 76, 79,
 88, 90, 139–41
parties, 39–40, 51–2, 76, 79–90, 99,
 112, 122, 130, 133, 140–1, 148
plebeian nations, 21, 27
plebeian peasant nations, 23–4
Poland ,4–5, 7, 10–11, 19, 30–1, 37, 39,
 42–4, 56–8, 61–3, 65, 70–2, 74–7,
 80, 87, 89, 94–5, 106, 109–11, 115,
 121–3, 130–1, 135–8, 147–8, 150–1
Poles, 29, 31–2, 111, 126
Polish, 18–19, 27, 30, 32, 37–8, 50, 62,
 80, 88, 123
Polish imperial nationalism, 19
Polish landowners in Ukraine and
 Belarus, 21
Polish nationalism, 18, 20, 27, 29;
 strong 28
political development, democratic,
 28–9, 36
political forces, anti-liberal, 80,
 84, 92
political parties, 38, 57, 90, 101, 127,
 142, 144, 150
political systems, 1, 47, 121, 135, 141
popularism, 84, 89–91
population, 5–6, 15, 32, 38, 73, 95–8,
 102, 105, 107, 116–17, 121–2, 138,
 142–3, 148
populism, 64, 84, 91, 150–1
populists, 81, 85, 88, 150–1
post-communist era, 5–6, 67, 134
post-communist states, 5, 103, 109
Prawo i Sprawiedliwość (PiS) party,
 80, 88, 138
Prussia, 13, 18, 20, 27
Public Management Theory, 4, 103–4,
 112, 142
Putin, Vladimir, 7, 124–30

Qaeda (al), 6, 12, 107, 113–15, 117
quotas, 107–10, 147, 149

reforms, 27, 70, 75; genuine land, 26;
 market, 76; political, 75; radical
 land, 36
refugee flow, 8, 108, 147
refugees, 6, 8, 66, 78, 104–5, 107–11,
 148–9
regime, semi-authoritarian, 35, 38, 41
resources, 21, 43, 55, 61
revolutions, 5, 18, 32, 34, 51, 64;
 liberal, 65; post-WWI, 36; second
 industrial, 15; social, 20
right-wing ideologies, 76, 85
rights: civil, 65; ethnic minority, 151
Roma, 100, 104, 109, 116
Roma Muslim, 120
Roma people, 6
Romania, 20, 26–7, 30, 40–2, 45–8,
 54–8, 61–5, 71–2, 74–80, 86–7,
 98–9, 102, 105–6, 109–11, 115, 117,
 123, 131, 134–6, 140, 150
Romanians, 18, 24, 32, 41, 59, 79, 86,
 102, 106
Russia, 7, 9, 13–16, 18, 23, 25–30, 32,
 35, 77, 86–7, 90, 94–5, 100, 102,
 105, 107, 121, 123–9, 131–3, 145,
 148, 151
Russian aggression, 102, 132
Russian culture, 102, 128
Russian history, 128, 133
Russian influence, 1, 102
Russian invasion, 132, 134
Russian invasion of Ukraine, 1, 94,
 110, 123, 131, 133
Russian minorities, 6, 90, 93–5,
 101–2, 126
Russian takeover of Crimea, 94,
 124, 129
Russian threat, 7, 123, 126
Russian troops, 124, 126
Russians, 5, 13, 15, 26, 30, 37, 48, 60,
 94–5, 103, 105, 110, 123–5, 129, 134,
 144, 147

Sachs, Jeffrey, 77–8
San Stefano, Treaty of, 25
secession, 25, 56, 68
security, 1, 12, 95, 108, 113, 116, 119,
 121–2, 133; domestic, 113, 118

# Index

Serbia, 23, 25–8, 30, 32, 35, 59, 68, 71, 75–7, 79–80, 84–7, 96, 98, 100, 103, 109, 131, 135
Serbian, 23–4, 32, 59, 96
Serbs, 18, 23–4, 31–2, 39, 48, 59, 67–8, 85, 96–8, 100, 115, 117–19, 141
serfdom, 14–15, 19, 23, 72
Sevastopol, 123–4, 128
Slovakia, 21–3, 46–8, 60, 71, 72, 74, 76–7, 87, 89, 98–9, 104, 106, 109–11, 117, 131, 135, 138
Slovaks, 18, 22–3, 31–2, 38, 56, 59, 76, 151
Slovenia, 66, 68, 71–2, 74–5, 77, 80, 87, 89, 99, 106, 108, 115, 131, 135–8
Slovenians, 24, 31, 59
social structures, 17, 23, 26, 35, 38
socialism, 50–1, 53–5, 61, 73
societies, 20, 52, 73, 75, 149
soldiers, 47, 60, 63, 117, 124, 145
South Korea, 78
South Ossetia, 102, 128
Southeast Europe, 116, 135
Soviet and allied military intervention, 61
Soviet Empire, 52, 55, 59, 61–2, 64–5
Soviet Empire in Eastern Europe, 50, 56
Soviet invasion, 37, 55
Soviet Union, 3, 20, 31, 34, 44–6, 49–51, 54–9, 61, 64–5, 94, 101, 105, 123, 145; former 57, 72, 78, 125
Soviets, 10, 45, 51, 54, 56–8, 60–2
Srebrenica Massacre, 97, 117, 150
Sri Lanka, 106, 120
Stabilisation Force (SFOR), 97, 118
stability, 11, 63, 96, 101, 107, 113, 133
Stalin, 20, 50, 55, 57
Stalinism, 57–58, 60–1
states, recipient, 108, 111–12
Strategic Concept, 133; new NATO, 132
Syria, 7, 104, 107–8, 120, 150
system, global capitalist, 33, 63
Systems Theory, 4, 113, 122

Taliban, 117
terrorism, 7, 114–16, 118–19, 150–1

terrorist acts, 115, 121
terrorist attacks, 120
terrorists, 6, 114, 117, 150
Third Reich, 43, 45
Thrace, 27–8
Tito, Josip Broz, 58–9
Trans-Carpathian Ukraine, 56
Transdniestrian Russian minority, 101
Transdniestrian Russians, 93
Transdniestrian territory of Moldova, 102
Transparency International Corruption Perception Index, 87
Transylvania, 21, 27, 41, 57–8
Treaty of Berlin, 25–6
Trianon Peace Treaty, 20
Trump, Donald, 92
Trumpism, 84
Tuđman, Franjo, 79, 89
Turkey, 58, 78, 103, 108, 120, 132
Turkish minority, 102

Ukraine, 1, 3, 5, 7, 43, 46, 70–1, 74, 77, 86–7, 94, 102, 104–5, 110–12, 120, 123–34, 143, 145, 147, 151
Ukrainian Refugees, 110, 126
Ukrainians, 7, 18–19, 30–1, 37, 43, 47, 110–11, 125, 148
United Nations Protection Force (UNPROFOR), 97, 117
United States, 30, 33–4, 42, 44–6, 51, 64, 67, 84, 91–2, 98, 101, 107, 110, 114, 119, 144, 147
Uzbekistan, 127

Versailles, Peace Treaty and order, 25–6, 31, 42–3, 56
violence, 5, 7, 36, 38, 41, 65, 115, 119; interethnic, 39, 48; organized, 65
Visegrad Four, 109
Vojvodina, 23, 27, 59

Wales Summit, NATO, 129
warfare, 28, 32
Warsaw Treaty Organization (WTO), 10, 56, 65, 123, 145

## Index

Washington Treaty, 133
Western Europe, 13, 15–16, 32, 48, 69–70, 78
Western European, 13–14, 28, 44, 47, 66, 69, 78
Western institutions, 75–6, 78, 90
women's suffrage, 37
World War I (WWI), 4, 5, 8–10, 19–20, 22–3, 27, 30, 33–5, 40, 44, 49, 93, 136, 143–4, 146

World War II (WWII), 2, 15, 19–20, 32, 51, 56, 58, 66, 111

Yugoslavia, 20, 24, 30–1, 39, 42, 45, 49, 51–2, 54, 56–64, 71, 96–7, 99, 103, 105–6, 115, 119, 121; communist, 39, 57, 60, 68
Yugoslavian succession, wars of, 64, 66

Zelenskyy, Volodimir, 132